THE WAY OF THE CROSS

FOLLOWING JESUS
IN THE GOSPEL OF MARK

Joel B. Green

DISCIPLESHIP RESOURCES
MATERIALS FOR GROWTH IN CHRISTIAN FAITH AND LIFE
P.O. Box 189 • Nashville, TN 37202 • Phone (615) 340-7284

Unless otherwise indicated, all scripture quotations are taken from the New Revised Standard Version of the Holy Bible. Copyright © 1989 by the Division of Christian Education of the National Council of Churches of Christ in the USA and used by permission.

Library of Congress Card Catalog No. 91-71794

ISBN 0-88177-103-1

DR103B

TO MARTA

GUIDE ON THE
VIA DOLOROSA

CONTENTS

PREFACE

All but the most skeptical of historians affirm the historical reality of the crucifixion of Jesus under Pontius Pilate.[1] Christians, however, have never been content with a mere affirmation of the *fact* of Jesus' execution. Christians want to know, What is the *meaning* of this event? What does the cross tell us about Jesus? About God's care for humanity? About God's purpose in the world? About the character of Christian discipleship? These are not only our questions; Mark the Evangelist addressed them in his story of Jesus, written in the mid-first century.

Why is the riddle of Jesus' passion and death so important to us? Undoubtedly, Christians are drawn to the cross in part because of longstanding debates surrounding its relation to God's saving purpose for the world. Perhaps there is another reason: The question of the suffering of the Son of God raises profound questions about our own suffering—and this is an aspect of life that touches us all.

This study focuses on the meaning of the cross in the Gospel of Mark. As such it embraces, above all, the relation of Jesus' mission—with its orientation to the cross—to the nature of discipleship. Key to this relationship for Mark is "the way of the Lord," introduced in Mark 1:1-3, developed later in the Gospel as the way of Jesus, the way of the cross, the way of discipleship. Following Jesus on "the way"—this is the invitation to discipleship, and this is its content.

My concern with the significance of Jesus' crucifixion is rooted in my postgraduate research on the death of Jesus at the University of Aberdeen. My own pastoral work during that period in the Northeast of Scotland Mission Circuit, together with the example of my supervisor, I. Howard Marshall—professor and British Methodist pastor, for whom building bridges between technical scholarship and the local church is a matter of course—nudged me always to consider the implications of my studies for everyday discipleship. Although that period of study resulted in a study of a very different sort than this one,[2] that exploration of earliest interpretations of the cross of Christ helped me realize the variety of lines along which the tradition developed.

My work then focused on the account of Jesus' suffering and death in the earliest church and in our Gospels, but it also led me to a later exploration of a different sort of "narrative."[3] This was the story of persecution and martyrdom, as followers of Jesus already in the apostolic church told the tale of their own suffering against the backdrop of the suffering of their Lord. This is in part the story of the Gospel of Mark, but it is shared with other New Testament authors and writings, including Paul, Hebrews, 1 Peter, Revelation, and, in its own way, Luke-Acts.

Reflection on biblical texts is always an interactive affair, and I am happy to record my debt to some of those who have helped shape my own reflection on the issues raised in this book. In her commitment to "the other," in her own sickness, and more recently in the pain arising from relative isolation, Marta Russell has helped point out to me the way of the cross. With deep respect and appreciation for her friendship I dedicate this study to her. My students at New College for Advanced Christian Studies, Berkeley, and especially Diane Clarke and Dana Parker, have been important conversation partners in coming to terms with the cross in the New Testament. My friendships with Mark Lau Branson and William A. Dyrness; my engagement with the Berkeley Emergency Food Project; and above all my family, Pamela, Aaron, and Allison, have all helped push the boundaries of my understanding of "the way."

Joel B. Green
New College Berkeley
Epiphany 1991

CHAPTER ONE

WHY HAVE YOU FORSAKEN ME?

[T]he chief priests, along with the scribes, were also mocking [Jesus] among themselves and saying, "He saved others; he cannot save himself. Let the Messiah, the King of Israel, come down from the cross now, so that we may see and believe." Those who were crucified with him also taunted him.

When it was noon, darkness came over the whole land until three in the afternoon. At three o'clock Jesus cried out with a loud voice, "Eloi, Eloi, lema sabachthani?" which means, "My God, my God, why have you forsaken me?" Mark 15:31-34.

When we said our goodbye's just before we left the country in 1982, she was the picture of wellness. And why not? When I met her six years earlier, Jo was already living the American Dream. She had a wonderful husband, two all-American children, a comfortable home in the suburbs. She was the resident mother-in-the-faith for hordes of young people in her church. Her own disciplined life of prayer and Bible study had become a fountain of nourishment for her and others. She was healthy; she had the gift of youthful looks. Jo had given her life to following Jesus; had God not honored her commitment by giving her friends, peace and stability, wholeness? So it seemed in the summer of '82.

Only months later, her dream turned into a nightmare. One afternoon, on an outing with her family, she had a seizure. This one led to others, and they were all inexplicable. For the next three years she would pass from one hospital, one specialized clinic, to another. But the word was always the same. Physicians would rub their chins, shake their heads, shrug their shoulders; none could give her an answer. Her seizures had no apparent cause or cure. They were a mystery. What could they be?

Her Christian friends were not caught by surprise, however. For them, there were no mysteries. They knew what the problem must be—both the cause and the cure. One by one, they shared their diagnoses with Jo and her family.

One said, "Obviously, you have somehow opened your life to demonic influence. When will you allow us to have a service of exorcism?"

Another wondered, "What have you done wrong, Jo? What sin are you hiding from us?"

Still another insisted, "Jo, I've been telling you for years that you were not properly submitted to your husband! And now your life of disobedience has caught up with you."

We can almost hear Job's friends in the distance. Having heard of all the troubles that had come upon Job, they decided to visit him, to offer their sympathy. Nothing could have prepared them for the pain they witnessed when they found him, however. They began to doubt their friend. They could not believe Job could be upright before God, yet suffer so much. One of Job's friends, Eliphaz the Temanite, sets forth the case as follows:

> Think now, who that was innocent ever perished?
>   Or where were the upright cut off?
> As I have seen, those who plow iniquity
>   and sow trouble reap the same.
> By the breath of God they perish,
>   and by the blast of his anger they are consumed (Job 4:7-9).

Later, Bildad the Shuhite adds his voice:

> If you will seek God
>   and make supplication to the Almighty,
> if you are pure and upright,
>   surely then he will rouse himself for you
>   and restore to you your rightful place (Job 8:5-6).

Eliphaz, Bildad, and Zophar—they had all come to comfort Job. Having arrived and witnessed the extent of his suffering, Job's friends can only assure him that his guilt has attracted divine punishment. Those who are right before God, they insist, do not suffer. They cannot believe Job is innocent; his pain is too great.

Job and our friend Jo are not alone, of course. The Old and New Testaments repeatedly narrate the stories of people who are committed to God, upright before God, yet experience sometimes heinous suffering. Luke opens his Gospel with the story of Elizabeth and Zechariah. They were, he writes, "righteous before God, living blamelessly according to all the commandments and regulations of the Lord. But they had no children . . ." (Luke 1:6-7). In a culture where God's blessing was understood to consist in part in the provision of children, Elizabeth and Zechariah had long suffered shame in their own community (Luke 1:25, 58). Theirs was no life-threatening situation, but the contrast between their faithfulness before God and their condition of childlessness is striking.

Other stories continue the drama of the suffering of the righteous. Early in the Christian mission, Stephen is stoned to death, just as all of God's righteous prophets before him had been (Acts 7:52-60). While on the cross, Jesus is mocked: If he is the Messiah, what is he doing on this cross?

Of course, this is not the side of life we want to talk about. We live in a time when everyone's goal is to be happy and healthy. If it is not fun, why keep doing it? "Don't worry, be happy." And if any of us fail to live up to these standards, we become problems to be solved quickly, or else abandoned and avoided. Thus, discussions revolving around pain are out-of-bounds at our dinner parties; our songs should be joyous ones, our greetings pleasant. We live out our agonies secretly, vicariously through the misfortunes of others, played out for us on television talk shows. As Charles Taylor writes in the conclusion of his profound study of the making of the modern identity, folks today place a high priority on the avoidance of death and suffering.[1]

If this is true for society-at-large, it is all the more true for many Christian believers. People who suffer are an embarrassment to our faith, to our understanding of our gracious God. If our God is benevolent, if God is omnipotent, could not, should not this God intervene to dispense with human suffering? And what of the suffering of Christians? Should not our belief in God put us on the winning side of history?[2] People in pain are enigmas. We want to put them and their anguish under lock and key, out of sight and out of mind, far away from our everyday lives.

So, Jesus' death cry in Mark's Gospel, "My God, my God, why have you forsaken me?" (15:34), is an embarrassment to us. We find ourselves naturally, unthinkingly gravitating toward Luke's account of the crucifixion. There Jesus' last words underscore the closeness of his relationship with God, even in death: "Father, into your hands I commend my spirit" (23:46). Even better is the last utterance of Jesus in John's Gospel—one word in Greek, *tetelestai,* "It is finished!" (19:30). Here, we may think, is a death cry befitting God's Messiah; we hear it as a word of triumph, interpreting Jesus' death as somehow the capstone of his life-bringing mission.

We are not the first ones to draw back from this cry of dereliction, this profound admission of loneliness in the midst of pain. Jesus' death cry in the Gospel of Mark, borrowed from Psalm 22:1 by Jesus, was offensive to the earliest Christian communities, too. For example, one very early copy and some early versions of this section of the Gospel of Mark substitute an alternative word for the problematic *forsaken.*[3] In these manuscripts, Jesus' last words read, "My God, my God, why have you *dishonored* me?"

Moreover, assuming with most students of the Gospels that Luke knew and used the Gospel of Mark as a source, Luke has clearly chosen not to include Mark's cry of dereliction in his story of Jesus' execution.

What Jesus *said* at his death was not the only problem—or even the first problem—for those earliest Christians, however. More pressing was the fact that Jesus had died on a cross at all. As Paul notes in his correspondence with the believers at Corinth, "Christ crucified" was "a stumbling block to Jews and foolishness to Gentiles" (1 Cor. 1:23). In writing these words, Paul was giving testimony to the hard realities of the scandal of the message of the cross in the ancient Roman world. This scandal is rooted in four interrelated ways of thinking in the first century.

First, within the Old Testament and later Jewish tradition, God had repeatedly intervened on behalf of faithful people, saving them *from* death. Perhaps the two best-known stories of God's delivering faithful people from death are recorded in the Old Testament book of Daniel. The first, in Daniel 3, narrates how Daniel's friends, Shadrach, Meshach, and Abednego, were bound and thrown into a furnace of blazing fire. The flames were so hot, we are told, that they killed the men who threw Daniel's friends into the fire. Nevertheless, of Shadrach, Meshach, and Abednego it is reported, "the fire had [no] . . . power over the bodies of those men; the hair of their heads was not singed, their tunics were not harmed, and not even the smell of fire came from them" (3:27). God had delivered them from death.

Daniel himself is the chief character in the second story, told in Daniel 6. Because of his continuing to say his prayers three times each day, Daniel was thrown into the den of lions. The next day, the narrator tells us, "Daniel was taken up out of the den, and no kind of harm was found on him, because he had trusted in his God" (6:23).

These two stories share a common theme with many other similar stories: the rescue from death and exoneration of faithful men and women. Given the prevalence of this theme, we are not surprised when we read in Mark's story of Jesus' suffering and death that the Jewish leaders looked to see whether Jesus would descend from the cross. If he were innocent, if he were God's Messiah, would God not rescue him from death?

Second, crucifixion was an especially heinous mode of execution.[4] Because the act of crucifixion itself damaged no vital organs and caused no excessive bleeding, the process of dying was extended. Death came slowly, painfully, the result of asphyxiation or shock. The victim of crucifixion was displayed naked on the cross, ordinarily at a public crossroads, and was the object of public ridicule. As a final disgrace, the corpses of those crucified were almost always denied burial. How could God's Messiah have experienced such a brutal form of death?

Some modern Christians might question how pervasive this problem would have been within first-century Judaism. After all, from earliest times, following Jesus' own lead, Christians have found in Isaiah 52:13–53:12 a prophetic basis for the suffering of the Christ:

> [The Servant of the Lord] had no form or majesty that we should look at him, nothing in his appearance that we should desire him. He was despised and rejected by others; a man of suffering and acquainted with infirmity; and as one from whom others hide their faces he was despised, and we held him of no account (Isa. 53:2-3).

Why, then, we might ask, should first-century Jews be surprised by the suffering of God's Messiah; was it not foretold by the prophet Isaiah? What we must realize is that the Book of Isaiah itself never identifies the Servant of the Lord as God's Messiah. Nor do we find in ancient Judaism any interpretive tradition rooting Jewish messianic hopes in Isaiah's Suffering Servant. Even though messianic expectations were much more variegated than we often recognize, the Jewish historian Geza Vermes has pointed out that the primary portrait of the expected Messiah in Judaism before the time of Jesus was "a king of David's lineage, victor over the Gentiles, saviour and restorer of Israel." 5 Hopes of this nature allowed no room for suffering, so that the tragic, abhorrent death of Jesus raised sobering questions against his messianic status.

Third, within the Jewish tradition, "crucified" was equated with "cursed" by the time of Jesus. According to Deuteronomy 21:22-23,

> When someone is convicted of a crime punishable by death and is executed, and you hang him on a tree, his corpse must not remain all night upon the tree; you shall bury him that same day, for anyone hung on a tree is under God's curse.

In its original, historical context, this passage would have referred to the practice of impaling a body on a tree for public display *after* execution. It also highlights the importance of burial for Israel. As texts found at Qumran point out, however, by the first century Jews had found in Deuteronomy 21:22-23 a reference to crucifixion.6 Not only were victims of crucifixion publicly shamed, then, they were also divinely cursed. How could God's Messiah have been crucified? How could God's Messiah bear God's curse?

Fourth, Gentiles, non-Jewish people of the Greco-Roman world, also would have found offensive the message of a crucified Messiah. Such a horrific execution could hardly have happened to a divine being. In fact, in later years some would-be Gentile Christians retreated from the scandal of the crucifixion by denying that the Christ had actually died on the cross. For them, Jesus should have demonstrated his divinity by escaping from the cross. This idea may lie behind a story of Jesus' death written about A.D. 125 where, at the moment of his death, the Lord was taken up from the cross.[7]

As represented in the New Testament, earliest Christians refused to downplay the actuality of Jesus' crucifixion. For them, the suffering of Christ was not an enigma to be relegated to the periphery of their faith. Thus, a number of New Testament passages borrow words from Deuteronomy 21:22-23 by way of describing the method of Jesus' execution. Instead of referring to "the cross," Acts 5:30 notes how certain Jewish leaders had Jesus killed "by hanging him on a tree." Although our English translations do not always show it, other passages use similar language to indicate Jesus' death on a "tree" (see Luke 23:39; Acts 10:39; 13:29; Gal. 3:13; 1 Pet. 2:24). Why go to such lengths to root Jesus' death in Deuteronomy 21:22-23, a text that seems to have suggested to many that Jesus was the object of a divine curse? Far from hiding the fact of Jesus' crucifixion and its interpretation as a curse among some Jews, those early Christians highlighted it.

The suffering of Christ was too central a reality to those first Christians and their opponents; Jesus' followers had to address its significance straightforwardly. Somehow, they had to come to terms with this event, interpreting it within the framework of God's redemptive purpose. They recognized the cardinal importance of showing that the expression "Christ crucified" was not a contradiction in terms.

How has the Christian church in North America today dealt with the stigma of Jesus' crucifixion? Our unease with suffering in general may serve as an important hint of our tendency to draw back from the ignominy of Jesus' execution. Some of us, perhaps, are drawn in our suffering to the Son of God who suffers as we do (Mark 15:33-39). On the other hand, our traditions of interpretation more often than not move the spotlight away from the passion of Christ.

What is at the center of discussion, especially in Protestant churches, when the subject of the crucified Messiah is raised? When we explore the significance of the death of Jesus, we are ordinarily concerned with understanding how "Christ died for our sins."[8] The history of Christianity is dotted with attempts to clarify the mechanism by which Jesus' death brought about the forgiveness of sins. Numerous New Testament witnesses attest to the importance of this interpretation of Jesus' crucifixion. Paul in particular regards the formula, "Christ died for our sins in accordance with the scriptures," as integral to the earliest testimony of the Christian movement (1 Cor. 15:3-5). He refers to it repeatedly (see Rom. 4:25; 5:6; 8:32; Gal. 1:4; 2:20-21; 1 Thess. 5:9-10; et al.), as do other early Christian witnesses (see, for example, Heb. 1:3; 2:17; 1 Pet. 1:18-21; 2:21-25; 1 John 2:1-2). Even Luke, who has little apparent interest in the atonement, nevertheless narrates two episodes in which the death of Jesus is interpreted along these lines—the first at the Last Supper (Luke 22:19-20), and the second in Paul's farewell address to the leaders of the church at Ephesus (Acts 20:28).[9] Recent study has indicated that this interpretation of Jesus' death—namely, that God's salvation of humanity is grounded in this act—arises from Jesus' own interpretation of his death at the Last Supper.[10]

The importance of the atoning significance of Jesus' crucifixion for the message of the New Testament has given rise to a long-standing debate. How has Jesus' death procured salvation? Should Jesus' death be understood as his victory over demonic powers? As a profound demonstration to humanity of God's unsurpassed love? As the means by which the barrier between humanity and God could be removed? Overlooked in this fascination with theories of how Christ's work on the cross was effective for humanity are myriad other interpretations given Jesus' death already in the New Testament. Many of these reorient our attention away from the stratospheres of classical theories of the atonement to focus more centrally on the suffering of Jesus and the relation of his suffering to the suffering of believers—indeed, to the suffering of the world.

It may seem ironic that the exploration of a particular interpretation of the death of Jesus has actually served to draw our attention away from that death. Just as ironic is the reality that the Christian celebration of Jesus' resurrection has tended to overshadow contemplation of the cross of Christ. Again, this is not to suggest the message of Jesus' resurrection should be downplayed. From earliest times, Christians affirmed Jesus as Lord, a designation grounded in their experience of the resurrected Christ and their conviction that God had raised Jesus from the dead (see, for example, Acts 2:14-36). At the same time we must be careful how we work out the relationship between death and resurrection in the case of Jesus. Some see the cross as an enigma, an embarrassment that cried out to be overturned by the resurrection. For them, the death of Jesus was a wrong needing to be put right; the resurrection of Christ happened in spite of the ugliness of the crucifixion of Jesus of Nazareth. This, they assume, is the proper meaning of the notion that in his resurrection Jesus was vindicated by God.

Such a view understandably moves our focal point away from the cross. Accordingly, we find ourselves somewhat ambivalent about the church calendar; our instincts motivate us to look beyond Lent, beyond Maundy Thursday, beyond Good Friday to the good news of the resurrection of Jesus from the dead. Rather than reflecting on the journey to Golgotha, our thoughts move ahead to Easter Morning; rather than dwelling on images of the Place of the Skull, our imaginations ponder scenes of the empty tomb. The passion of Christ is beyond our vision, hidden in the shadows beyond the brilliance of resurrection light.

Of course, this understanding of the resurrection as key to overturning the debacle of Jesus' execution has some merit. As the two travelers on the road to Emmaus demonstrate, for many, Jesus' crucifixion did raise important questions about his mission (Luke 24:19-21): If Jesus was found guilty in public trial and executed as a pretender to the throne, what are we to say about his public ministry? Did he really speak for God? Against such questions, the resurrection affirms the divine origins of Jesus' mission.

This is not the whole story, however. One might better insist that the resurrection authenticated the message of Jesus, not *in spite of* the cross, but *including* the message of his death on the cross. As we shall see, the Gospel of Mark in particular portrays the cross of Christ as the culmination of his mission.

How has the Christian church in North America today dealt with the stigma of Jesus' crucifixion? This is the question to which we addressed ourselves, but now we realize the necessity of raising a prior question: Have we yet recognized the stigma of Jesus' crucifixion? Has "Christ crucified" become for us a stumbling block, a folly? Have we felt the depth of Jesus' cry from the cross, "My God, my God, why have you forsaken me?" Have we come face to face with the brutality of Jesus' crucifixion? Have we comprehended the strange paradox of the suffering of the righteous as represented ultimately in the pain of Jesus' trial and execution? For many, traditional ways of interpreting the cross and resurrection will have worked to dull our sensitivity to these matters. And this is doubly unfortunate. Not only has it distanced us from the passion of Christ as a primary component of the New Testament message, but it has also robbed us of a key means for coming to grips with our own pain and our understanding of the meaning of discipleship. Can we find in the Gospel of Mark a resource for the rediscovery of the message of the cross, the way of discipleship?

The body of the Gospel of Mark does not name its author, though since the beginning of the second century this writing has been associated with the name of Mark. Nor does the Gospel give any clear indication of its audience. Undoubtedly, however, Mark's first-century readers and hearers were not unlike those of us in the twentieth century who turn to his Gospel for encouragement and direction. As we shall see, Mark's audience was a perplexed people. They were a people with well-established beliefs and convictions about the nature of God's kingdom,[11] about the character and activity of God's agent of salvation, about the life of discipleship. But a great chasm had opened between their faith-grounded expectations and the realities of their world. God's kingdom had not come in fullness, in power. God's agent of salvation, the Messiah, had been crucified, not crowned. And the way of discipleship had become not a life of bliss, but of duress.

For these people, Mark wrote what has been taken by some students of the Gospels as a passion story with an extended introduction. This assessment downplays too much the importance of the first thirteen chapters of Mark's Gospel for one's understanding of the Gospel as a whole. It does, however, underscore the prominence of the death of Jesus in the message of the Gospel. For Mark, we have not understood Jesus if we have not plumbed the depths of his passion. Clearly, Mark believes that authentic discipleship must be oriented to the cross, and that followers of Jesus must join him on the way of the cross.

Questions for Reflection and Discussion

1. How does your church or fellowship look at suffering?

2. How do we pray about suffering?

3. How does our experience of suffering shape our view of God?

4. How does our experience of God shape our view of suffering?

5. What beliefs do we hold that might draw our attention away from the significance of suffering?

CHAPTER TWO

THE MINISTRY OF JESUS:
A STORY OF SUCCESS?

> *They went to Capernaum; and when the sabbath came, [Jesus]*
> *entered the synagogue and taught. They were astounded at his*
> *teaching, for he taught them as one having authority, and not as*
> *the scribes. Just then there was in their synagogue a man with an*
> *unclean spirit, and he cried out, "What have you to do with us,*
> *Jesus of Nazareth? Have you come to destroy us? I know who*
> *you are, the Holy One of God." But Jesus rebuked him, saying,*
> *"Be silent, and come out of him!" And the unclean spirit,*
> *convulsing him and crying with a loud voice, came out of him.*
> *They were all amazed, and they kept on asking one another,*
> *"What is this? A new teaching—with authority! He commands*
> *even the unclean spirits, and they obey him." At once his fame*
> *began to spread throughout the surrounding region of Galilee*
> *(Mark 1:21-28).*

What is the significance of Jesus of Nazareth? Christians throughout history have explored this question using numerous instruments. Songs have been sung, statements of faith penned, scenes from his life reenacted, sermons preached, the Lord's Supper celebrated, portraits painted. These and hosts of other media have probed the meaning of the ministry of Jesus of Nazareth. Many of these were used already by the earliest Christians, who formed simple creeds, such as "Jesus is Lord" (Rom. 10:9), and developed hymns to Christ, such as that found in Philippians 2:6-11. Paul's letters in the New Testament constitute the earliest extant written communication drawing out the significance of Jesus. It is widely agreed that this form of literature, the letter, was well suited to Paul's need to deal with specific, concrete issues among local Christian gatherings.

Only later, in the A.D. 60s, was the significance of Jesus explored in story form, in what we today call a "Gospel." This raises an important question.

If letters such as 1 Corinthians and 1 Thessalonians were helpful for treating the needs of local Christian communities, what need prompted the development of the narrative of Jesus' life and ministry? What exigencies led to Mark's sketching the life of Jesus in story format? If Mark had other options available to him for communicating the significance of Jesus of Nazareth to his audience, why did he choose to write the story of this man? This is a particularly pointed question because it is widely held today that Mark wrote the first Gospel. That is, "Gospel writing" was not among the well-known options readily available to him; he had to create this form of literature by borrowing from other types of literature in his world.

We might reflect on this question by raising it in a more general way: What do stories do well? Several answers come to mind.[1] First, they encourage in the audience a sense of affinity with the central character or characters of the story. Second, they show the rich interrelatedness among the many forces that help shape human experience in concrete situations. Third, they draw their audiences into new worlds in order to further undergird or to challenge the way readers and hearers think and act.

Any reading of the Gospel of Mark will point out the appropriateness to Mark's project of these first two descriptions of the contribution of narrative. Mark clearly invites his audience to identify with Jesus and, to a lesser degree, to wonder about the role of the disciples. Moreover, he portrays numerous forces, some mundane and personal, others cosmic, that together shape the lives of the characters of the story.

What may be less transparent is how Mark might be inviting his readers into the story of Jesus in order to shape their own worlds. How might Mark be challenging or affirming the significance they attribute to Jesus; how might he be critiquing or embracing the perspectives and actions of his audience through his story? Our answer to this question may not be so clear—not because Mark is a poor author, but because we in North America at the end of the twentieth century are so far removed from the social realities of Mark's first-century readers. Our concerns, our lives are different from theirs. In order to appreciate Mark's agenda, we must undertake a close reading of the story, an exploration of *its* questions, *its* perspectives, the colors with which *it* paints the mural of Jesus' life, death, and resurrection. This may lead us into the story of Jesus more fully. For Mark's Gospel, one way to accomplish this is to focus especially on the identity of the main character, Jesus, and to investigate how others in the narrative relate to him. In fact, this is a key element of the story Mark tells.

WHO IS JESUS? THE PIVOTAL ISSUE

"Who do people say that I am?" Jesus asks his disciples. Coming as it does halfway through the Gospel of Mark (8:27), this question is clearly pivotal for the Gospel. Even more important, however, is the query that immediately follows: "But who do *you* say that I am?" (8:29).

On one level, this is an examination for Peter, James, John, and the others, those disciples chosen by Jesus who have participated as characters in the story of Jesus' mission. On another level, Jesus' inquiry reaches outside of the pages of the Gospel. The question, Who do you say that I am?, is no longer addressed only to his first disciples, but to Mark's readers and hearers, second and third generation disciples of Jesus. Having heard the stories, having encountered Jesus in the Gospel of Mark, what opinion have they formed of him? Who is this Jesus? What have they made of this man from Galilee?

Jesus' direct questions about himself in Mark 8 are not the first to be raised about his identity. Especially in the first half of the Gospel, the question appears repeatedly and in numerous forms. It is raised both explicitly and implicitly by a variety of characters.

Already in Mark 1, for example, in the context of Jesus' first ministry in a synagogue, the matter of his identity comes into focus. Here, in verses 21-28, Jesus enters Capernaum, the hub city of his ministry in Galilee. On the Sabbath he serves as the guest speaker, but his teaching is interrupted by the presence of a man with an unclean spirit. Jesus takes charge of the unclean spirit, commanding him to come out of the man.

Throughout this episode, the quality of Jesus' ministry electrifies his audience:

> They were astounded at his teaching, for he taught them as one having authority, and not as the scribes. . . . They were all amazed, and they kept on asking one another, "What is this? A new teaching—with authority! He commands even the unclean spirits, and they obey him" (Mark 1:22, 27).

Unlike the Gospels of Matthew and Luke, where the presentation of Jesus as teacher includes significant accounts of the substance of his teaching, the Gospel of Mark is more interested in the "that" (or fact) of his teaching than the "what" (that is, its content). In this episode, then, instead of providing a window into the content of Jesus' instruction, Mark underscores its authority. Mentioned twice in this story, Jesus' authority sets him apart from other teachers of his day. Rather than place his opinions alongside those of other learned people, building the argument of his sermon on the foundations of others' viewpoints, or sprinkling his address with the words of well-known experts, Jesus apparently sets forth his own interpretation of the Hebrew Scriptures as authoritative. This results not only in reactions of astonishment from the people, but also in his being recognized by an unclean spirit as "the Holy One of God" (1:24).

Jesus exhibits authority in his teaching as well as in his power over evil, and this raises the issue of his identity: "What is this?" the people ask. They recognize the quality of his ministry, but they do not know what to make of it. Their encounter with Jesus leads to amazement and puzzlement, but not to faith. They perceive his authority, but they do not comprehend its significance.

The next three appearances of the issue of Jesus' identity in the Gospel of Mark come in Chapter 2. In a series of stories related by their focus on Jesus' growing unpopularity with the Jewish leadership, we see the matter of his identity raised repeatedly in the midst of controversy. In the first story (2:1-12), a paralyzed man is lowered through the roof of the house where Jesus is teaching. Seeing him and the faith of his friends, Jesus says to the man, "Son, your sins are forgiven." Having heard this, the scribes wonder, "Why does this fellow speak in this way? It is blasphemy! Who can forgive sins but God alone?" (2:7). We might paraphrase their response, "Who does he think he is, that he should act in God's stead?" Jesus' reply is an affirmation of his authority on earth to forgive sins (2:10), and his healing of the paralytic. This encounter does not define clearly the connection between disease and sin, but it does demonstrate Jesus' powerful opposition to evil and its kin in any form as well as his understanding that salvation embraces health in all its forms. In embodying the good news in this way, Jesus assumes for himself divine prerogatives, and gives a concrete demonstration of his authority to forgive sins. Notice the response of the crowd gathered in the house: "We have never seen anything like this!"

This story is immediately followed by another, in which Jesus calls Levi the tax collector to discipleship, then sits down to eat with Levi and other tax collectors and sinners (2:13-17). As we will see more clearly in Chapter 4 of this book, Jesus' actions challenge religious and social conventions of his day related to table fellowship. This leads to another assertion of the identity issue: "Why does he eat with tax collectors and sinners?" (2:16). Jesus has been passing himself off as a teacher, an interpreter of the scriptures, an itinerant preacher. Should not a holy man of his stature disassociate himself from public riffraff? What sort of person is this?

Finally, in Mark 2:23-28, we read the story of Jesus' encounter with the Pharisees over the matter of breaking sabbath law. According to the narrative as Mark relates it, Jesus' disciples have been plucking heads of grain on the sabbath, a practice the Pharisees condemn on the basis of their reading of the sabbath law (see Exod. 20:8-11; Deut. 5:12-15). As their master-teacher, Jesus is responsible for the behavior of his disciples, so the query is put to him, "Look, why are they doing what is not lawful on the sabbath?" What sort of teacher is this, who lets his disciples countermand the law of Moses? Does he not take seriously the authority of the scriptures? Jesus replies with some biblical interpretation of his own, but the primary issue of the story revolves around a decision regarding his person (see also Mark 7:5). Does his mission take precedence over the command not to work on the sabbath? Has he the requisite authority to reinterpret the sabbath command?

Thus far, the question of Jesus' identity has been raised by onlookers and opponents. At the end of Mark 4, however, even his disciples fail to discern who he is. Mark 4 consists primarily of Jesus' teaching in parables, and Mark makes a point of telling his readers that Jesus has spent extra time spelling out their meaning to the disciples (4:10-20, 33-34). Will the disciples, then, understand? After a day of teaching in parables, Jesus and his disciples decide to cross over the Sea of Galilee in a boat. When they are overtaken by a storm, the disciples awaken Jesus with their pleas for help. Rising, he "rebuked the wind, and said to the sea, 'Peace, Be still!'" (4:39). The wind ceased and the sea became calm. How did the disciples respond? Mark writes, "And they were filled with great awe and said to one another, 'Who then is this, that even the wind and the sea obey him?'" (4:41).

The crowds, his opponents, even his disciples are unable to grasp Jesus' significance, in spite of the continuing record of his powerful deeds and growing popularity. They are not alone, however. Not even the people of Nazareth, his own hometown, or even King Herod can fathom his identity. Jesus returns to his hometown to teach, but the people can only respond in astonishment: "Where did this man get all this? What is this wisdom that has been given to him?" (6:1-6 [2]). What is the source of Jesus' ministry? By what authority does he teach and work miracles? Not his family or his childhood education, this is certain; his own family thinks he has lost his mind, and he is a common laborer (3:21, 31-35; 6:3). Who is this man? This very question seems to have been discussed in Herod's presence (6:14-16): Was he John, now raised from the dead? Elijah? Some other ancient prophet?

Who is Jesus? This brief survey of selected stories in the first half of Mark's Gospel demonstrates the central importance of this quandary for the Gospel as a whole. But finding an answer to this riddle is for Mark no mere speculative concern. Mark is not interested in identifying Jesus for the sake of producing the right answer; he is concerned with much, much more than getting his doctrines correct. Equally transparent is the related Markan concern with appropriate response to Jesus. As we have seen, how different characters respond to Jesus is a product of their perception of who he is. Amazement, fear, anger, bewilderment, confusion, unbelief—these are the kinds of responses to Jesus we have discovered thus far. Amazingly, even those closest to Jesus—his family and his disciples—respond in much the same way as everyone else. They do not understand. Something must be missing.

The question of Jesus' identity is central because it is so often misconstrued. In this, then, Mark's readers find themselves in the same position as the characters of his Gospel. In repeatedly echoing the question, Who is Jesus?, Mark invites his readers and hearers to ask this question themselves and to be open to having their images of Jesus transformed.

FIRST ANSWER: THE BEGINNING OF THE GOSPEL

In fact, from the outset Mark provides his own answer to the question, Who is Jesus? Within the story of Jesus' ministry, beginning in Mark 1:16, the people around Jesus are not always clear about Jesus' identity. Mark has given *his readers* inside information, however. The introduction to the Gospel, Mark 1:1-15, provides data about Jesus' significance directly to Mark's readers and hearers. Within the timeline of the story itself, though, this knowledge is unknown to Peter and the other disciples, Jesus' family, the Jewish leadership, the crowds, and other characters.

Mark provides the primary point of view for the identity of Jesus in his Gospel. He affirms that Jesus is the Christ, the Son of God, as was announced by the prophet Isaiah (1:1-3). Jesus' identity is then confirmed by God at his baptism—"You are my Son, the Beloved; with you I am well pleased" (1:11). In Mark's story, these divine words are heard only by Jesus; they are reported to Mark's readers but not to the other characters of the story.

What do we, Mark's readers, understand about Jesus that those around Jesus in Mark's story struggle to perceive? Jesus' identity, together with the content of Mark's Gospel, is made clear already in Mark 1:1-3. Unfortunately, the New Revised Standard Version has left unclear the function of Mark's opening verse. As this version has it, verse 1—"The beginning of the good news of Jesus Christ, the Son of God"—might serve as a heading or title for the whole story Mark tells. Alternatively, this "good news" might refer to the message preached by Jesus or even the message about Jesus. Moreover, the New Revised Standard Version ties the quotation from Isaiah directly to the ministry of John the baptizer. As a result, we are not sure how Isaiah's message or the work of John relates to "the beginning of the good news of Jesus Christ, the Son of God." We should remove these ambiguities by punctuating the text as follows:

> The beginning of the good news of Jesus Christ, the Son of
> God, as it is written in the prophet Isaiah:
> "See, I am sending my messenger ahead of you,
>   who will prepare your way;

the voice of one crying out in the wilderness:
'Prepare the way of the Lord,
make his paths straight.'"[2]

That is, Mark 1:1-15 is the "beginning of the good news of Jesus Christ, Son of God," and this "good news" is grounded in the message of Isaiah. The significance of Jesus is thus rooted in these titles, Christ and Son of God, and in Isaiah's message of the coming redemption of God's people. This is the information that Mark provides his readers at the outset; in this way, he orients them to understand Jesus' mission and message in a particular way. What is especially clear is how Mark wants us to read the significance of Jesus against the backdrop of the prophecy of Isaiah. Note the parallels he draws:

- The coming of John the baptizer (Mark 1:4-8; see Isa. 40)
- The baptism of Jesus (Mark 1:9-11; see Isa. 42:1; 61:1)
- Jesus in the wilderness (Mark 1:12-13; see Isa. 40; 65)
- Jesus' proclamation of the "good news of God" (Mark 1:14-15; see Isa. 40:9; 52:7; 61:1-2)

In short, Mark sees a profound connection between the promise of God's salvation in Isaiah and the good news of Jesus Christ. Jesus' significance is defined in part by the wonderful vision of God's coming redemption in Isaiah. Remember, though, this is "insider information." What the reader knows now, the characters within the story struggle to discover.

In other ways, Mark fills in our understanding of Jesus in these opening verses. John's message of repentance and Mark's report of the magnitude of the Jewish response to John (1:4-5) capitalize on the old belief that the age of redemption was contingent upon and might even be hastened by the repentance of all Israel.[3] Similarly, the promise of the baptism with the Holy Spirit (1:7-8) is grounded in the Old Testament anticipation of the outpouring of the Holy Spirit (see, for example, Ezek. 36:24-38; Joel 2:28-32). John's ministry helps identify Jesus as the one who will bring salvation.

Borrowing language from Psalm 2:7 and Isaiah 42:1-4, Mark's account of the baptism of Jesus (1:9-11) is cast as Jesus' coronation as the Anointed One, the Messiah, and as the Son of God. Having been anointed with the Holy Spirit, he is now ready to go forth as God's messenger, proclaiming good news (Isa. 61:1). Jesus' declaration of "the good news of God" is an announcement of the presence of God in the ministry of Jesus (see Isa. 40:9); Jesus heralds the presence of God's reign, of shalom (peace with justice), salvation (see Isa. 52:7). "The good news of Jesus Christ, Son of God," then, highlights Jesus as the one in whom the redemption of God has come to humanity. He is the bringer of the kingdom.

Jesus is the Christ. Jesus is the Son of God. Jesus is the bringer of God's salvation, the kingdom. This is clear enough, or is it? Are we really sure what it all means? It may be true that with regard to Jesus' identity the readers of Mark's Gospel have a head start on the characters in the story itself. It is equally clear, however, that Mark 1:1-15 lays out only the parameters for understanding who Jesus is. It does not provide decisive information as to the identity of Jesus and the character of his mission. Otherwise, we might wonder why Mark felt the need to tell the rest of the story.

Could it be that Mark's readers affirmed that Jesus was the Messiah, but misunderstood the nature of his messiahship? Could they have embraced his status as God's Son, but confused the nature of his Sonship? Could they have acknowledged Jesus as the kingdom bringer, but misconstrued the implications of that reality for their everyday lives? If Mark identifies Jesus so clearly in the opening section of his Gospel, why must the question "Who is Jesus?" be raised so frequently in the context of Jesus' mission as Mark relates it? Perhaps a second look is in order.

SECOND ANSWER: JESUS, THE POPULAR MIRACLE WORKER

What would happen if we attempted to answer Jesus' question, Who do you say that I am?, based solely on the portrait of Jesus available to us in the first half of the Gospel of Mark? No doubt, we would refer to Jesus as Christ, Son of God, and bringer of the kingdom of God, for Mark himself has given us this perspective in his opening verses. To give these answers, however, only begs the question, for we still need to know what it means for Jesus to be these things. How have these descriptions of Jesus in the introduction to the Gospel been filled out in the subsequent narrative?

What is the primary picture of Jesus in the first half of Mark's Gospel, 1:16–8:26? Above all else, Jesus is presented as a miracle worker who receives wide acclaim throughout the regions of his ministry. This perspective is evident in the major summaries of Jesus' mission in this part of the Gospel, where Mark highlights above all else the power of Jesus to cure diseases and to cast out demons. These summaries also speak in glowing terms of his growing popularity.

> That evening, at sundown, they brought to him all who were sick or possessed with demons. And the whole city was gathered around the door. And he cured many who were sick with various diseases, and cast out many demons (1:32-34).

> Jesus departed with his disciples to the sea, and a great multitude from Galilee followed him; hearing all that he was doing, they came to him in great numbers from Judea, Jerusalem, Idumea, beyond the Jordan, and

the region around Tyre and Sidon. He told his disciples to have a boat ready for him because of the crowd, so that they would not crush him; for he had cured many, so that all who had diseases pressed upon him to touch him (3:7-11).

When they had crossed over, they came to land at Gennesaret and moored the boat. When they got out of the boat, people at once recognized him, and rushed about that whole region and began to bring the sick on mats to wherever they heard he was. And wherever he went, into villages or cities or farms, they laid the sick in the marketplaces, and begged him that they might touch even the fringe of his cloak; and all who touched it were healed (6:53-56).

If the success of Jesus' ministry were evaluated in terms of public opinion, these summary statements would overwhelmingly tell the tale of his triumph. "The whole city"; "a great multitude from Galilee"; "in great numbers from Judea, Jerusalem, Idumea, beyond the Jordan, and the region around Tyre and Sidon"—these and similar descriptive words indicate the incredible popularity Jesus enjoyed during this stage of his ministry.[4] Mark 3:8 is particularly compelling in that Mark thus describes how people from the whole area of Jewish settlement in the Holy Land during the time of Jesus were excited about Jesus' mission. And why not? After all, he had been freeing people from demonic power and healing the sick. In fact, well over one-fourth of the whole Gospel is occupied with the miraculous activity of Jesus.

Jesus' power over cosmic forces is narrated repeatedly within the first half of Mark's Gospel. In addition to the story we have already examined in 1:23-27, Jesus performs exorcisms in 5:1-20 and 7:24-30. Moreover, he gives his disciples power to do the same (6:7), so that Mark's summary of their ministry highlights how they were able to cast out unclean spirits (6:13). Jesus' authority to cast out demons is questioned in 3:22-30, where the scribes from Jerusalem are of the opinion that "by the ruler of the demons he casts out demons." Jesus' reply interprets his earlier encounter with Satan in the wilderness (1:12): He is able to control demons because he has entered the house of the strong man (the devil) and plundered his house (3:27). Far from being in collusion with Satan, then, Jesus has brought close the power of God's reign against demonic forces.

Jesus' status as the conqueror of evil is manifest in a different way, too, in his miraculous quieting of the sea and his walking on the water (4:35-41; 6:47-52). Often, these stories are understood as portraying nature miracles, Jesus' ability to master the elements of this world. Much more is at work in these stories, however, though we must understand something about the symbolic meaning of "the sea" in Jewish antiquity to appreciate this larger meaning. In many contexts, of course, the sea represents nourishment and a means of travel. In others, this sea symbolizes chaos and evil. Some passages in the Old Testament portray God's mastery of the sea (for example, Pss. 65:7; 89:9; 106:9), while others go on to show how this mastery was exhibited in God's overcoming the sea as though it were a monstrous, evil power (Pss. 74:13-14; 104:4-9; 107:25-30). Revelation 21:1 picks up this motif in a different way, showing how the new heaven and new earth will be devoid of any sea (read: devoid of any evil).

Hence, when Jesus quiets the storm or walks on the water, he is not only acting as God acts, demonstrating mastery over the sea, but also manifesting his authority precisely over against the powers of evil. In the first episode, 4:35-41, this is also indicated by the words Jesus uses to quiet the storm. He *rebukes* the wind and *silences* the sea, just as he *rebukes* and *silences* demons (Mark 1:25; 3:11-12).

Jesus demonstrates his power in the context of cosmic forces, but also, repeatedly, in the physical healing of women, men, and children. Simon's mother-in-law is cured of a fever after Jesus "came and took her by the hand and lifted her up" (1:29-31). Moved with pity, Jesus cleanses a leper (1:40-45). He tells a paralytic, "Stand up, take your mat and go to your home," and the paralyzed man is enabled to do so (2:1-12). A man with a withered hand is cured on the sabbath (3:1-5). First a woman with a hemorrhage is healed, and then a daughter of a synagogue leader is brought back to life (5:21-43). A deaf man with a speech impediment is healed (7:31-35). And Jesus restores the sight of a blind man at Bethsaida (8:22-26). The crowds "are astounded beyond measure, saying, 'He has done everything well; he even makes the deaf to hear and the mute to speak'" (7:37).

Jesus' miraculous activity also embraces the feeding of the thousands, first with five loaves and two fish (6:33-44) and then with seven loaves and a few small fish (8:1-10). Some modern interpreters enjoy discussions about the mechanics of these miracles and suggest natural ways for these people to have received nourishment. Speculation of this nature is far from Mark's mind, however. Both stories highlight Jesus' compassion for the people, as well as his capacity to provide for them as shepherds provide for their sheep.

When we hear the question Jesus puts to his disciples, Who do you say that I am?, then, the answer seems clear enough. Jesus is a miracle worker with wide acclaim. He is a powerful healer with mastery over both natural and cosmic forces. His is a story of success, of popularity, of might. Through his powerful achievements he has conquered the forces of evil and gained nationwide prestige. Surely, we may think, this is what it means to be Christ, Son of God, kingdom bringer.

DO WE NEED ANOTHER LOOK?

But there is also a counter-melody. We can hear it above all in the last miracle story Mark recounts before turning to the crucial exchange between Jesus and his disciples on the subject of his identity in Mark 8.

> They came to Bethsaida. Some people brought a blind man to him and begged him to touch him. He took the blind man by the hand and led him out of the village; and when he had put saliva on his eyes and laid his hands on him, he asked him, "Can you see anything?" And the man looked up and said, "I can see people, but they look like trees, walking." Then Jesus laid his hands on his eyes again; and he looked intently and his sight was restored, and he saw everything clearly (Mark 8:22-25).

What separates this miracle story from others in the Gospel is that here the healing occurred in two stages. Although this episode can be added to the others demonstrating Jesus' healing power, it also functions for Mark as a kind of parable. The key to understanding how this story works for Mark is our recognition of the pervasive use of blindness as a metaphor for spiritual dullness. That is, this man's blindness symbolizes not only a physical ailment but also a spiritual condition, and not only his own condition but also that of the disciples. The disciples are unable to perceive Jesus' identity. Having received the "first touch," this man is able to see somewhat, just as the disciples have some appreciation of Jesus' nature and the character of his mission after having witnessed his powerful deeds. But theirs is only a limited perception; it is not enough for a full understanding of the character of Jesus and his ministry.

What more is needed? It is true that Jesus' deeds of power occupy the first half of Mark's Gospel, but this is not the whole story. Mark provides important hints of another reality, a counter-melody. Already in these opening chapters, Mark anticipates the cross.[5] Mark 2:18-20 narrates a dispute over fasting. Assuming that true piety is exhibited in fasting, some people come to Jesus to inquire why his disciples do not exercise this religious discipline. His answer takes the form of an analogy. Just as wedding guests do not fast in the presence of the bridegroom, so now, while Jesus is present, fasting is out of place. The surprising twist in this comparison appears in verse 20, where Jesus predicts a time when the bridegroom will be taken away. Jesus thus alludes to the time when he will be taken away suddenly and unexpectedly.

Mark 2:1–3:6 is a collection of stories that reflect the controversy stirred up by Jesus' ministry. Mark 3:6—"The Pharisees went out and immediately conspired with the Herodians against [Jesus], how to destroy him"—serves as the climax of this section. Both religious and political leaders, holding on to old priorities and resisting the grace extended through Jesus' ministry, have begun seeking his death. Jesus' mission demands human response, and their rejoinder is one of opposition—opposition that would lead to Jesus' violent death.

During his ministry among the people of his own hometown, Jesus quotes a well-known proverb with reference to himself: "Prophets are not without honor, except in their hometown, and among their own kin, and in their own house" (6:4). In this way he identifies with the fate of the prophets: rejection. Just as persecution and death were the fate of God's prophets of old (see, for example, Neh. 9:26; Jer. 2:30), so Jesus would meet rejection, suffering, and death.

The most developed anticipatory allusion to Jesus' death in the first half of Mark's Gospel is in the account of the death of John the baptizer (6:14-29). In retrospect, we can see how Mark connects the passion of John with that of Jesus. In both stories, Roman sympathy is shown for a prisoner who is innocent (6:20; 15:15); the death sentence is pronounced only under duress (6:26; 15:15); and, after death, disciples come, take the body, and lay it in a tomb (6:29; 15:42-47). The fates of John and Jesus were intertwined already in 1:14, where John's arrest led to the public ministry of Jesus. In Mark 6, both John and Jesus appear in the company of prophets and John joins the prophets in violent death. The fate of those like John and Jesus, who affirm the way of God even in the face of opposition, is transparent.

CONCLUSION

Already, Jesus the miracle worker is in trouble. The Christ may have far-reaching public support now, but the cross has already cast its shadow on the story of Jesus. He has not set out to find the cross, of course; Jesus is no masochist. Rather, he has embraced a lifestyle of compassion for others, of working in powerful though unconventional ways to free people from uncleanness, physical distress, demonic powers. This lifestyle has begun attracting opposition. Any answer to Jesus' question, Who do you say that I am?, must grapple with this reality.

Mark invites his readers into a quest to come to terms with who Jesus is in order that they might know how best to respond to him. On the surface of it, his story encourages us to identify Jesus as a powerful figure, popular and victorious over evil. His is a "successful" ministry. But this is a limited viewpoint. A second look is needed.

Questions for Reflection and Discussion

1. What opinion have people in your community formed of Jesus? On what basis have they come to these opinions?

2. In what ways are you attracted to the picture of Jesus we find in
   Mark 1-8? For people in your community, is this an attractive
   portrait? Why?

3. Have you seen the portrait of Jesus the miracle worker helpfully or hurtfully applied? Explain.

4. Jesus attracted opposition primarily from the religious and social leaders of his day. Why do you suppose this is true?

5. Do we expect that a Christian lifestyle will attract opposition today? Explain.

CHAPTER THREE

THE JOURNEY OF JESUS:
GOING TO GOLGOTHA

> *They were on the road, going up to Jerusalem, and Jesus was walking ahead of them; they were amazed, and those who followed were afraid. He took the twelve aside again and began to tell them what was going to happen to him, saying, "See, we are going up to Jerusalem, and the Son of Man will be handed over to the chief priests and the scribes, and they will condemn him to death; then they will hand him over to the Gentiles; they will mock him, and spit upon him, and flog him, and kill him; and after three days he will rise again"* (Mark 10:32-34).

Listen again to a well-known story:

Once upon a time in another land, a little boy reached the age when he could be given the responsibilities of a young shepherd. His task was to take his family's sheep out each morning so they might graze during the day on the back side of the mountain. Each evening he was to bring them home safely where they would be penned for the night.

Of course, the possibility of attack by wolves was always present. So, as he began his new chores, the little boy was instructed, "If you see a wolf, shout as loudly as you can, 'Wolf! Wolf!,' and we will come quickly to help you."

As the days wore on, the boy lost his initial excitement at having a real job. The sun was hot. He was all alone. He grew tired and bored. He decided to have a little fun, to play a joke on the people of his village. So, even though no danger was in sight, he shouted, "Wolf! Wolf!"

Quickly, the villagers came running, carrying sticks and shovels and other makeshift weapons, prepared to scare away the wolves before the flock could be eaten. But there was no wolf.

Seeing that they had been tricked, the townspeople scolded the boy and returned to their own work.

Day after day, the young boy returned with the sheep to the back side of the mountain so they might graze, and evening after evening he returned with the sheep to the village. As the days wore on, the boy forgot how angry the villagers had been at being tricked before. The sun was hot. He was all alone. He grew tired and bored. He decided to have a little fun, to play a joke on the people of his village. So, even though no danger was in sight, he shouted, "Wolf! Wolf!"

Quickly, the villagers came running, carrying sticks and shovels and other makeshift weapons, prepared to scare away the wolves before the flock could be eaten. But there was no wolf.

Seeing that they had been tricked again, they scolded the boy, then returned to their own work.

Day after day, the young boy returned with the sheep to the back side of the mountain so they might graze, and evening after evening he returned with the sheep to the village. Not many days later, however, a wolf did come—no, there were two! Terrified, the boy began to shout as loudly as he could, "Wolf! Wolf!"

But this time no one came running. No one brought sticks and shovels and other makeshift weapons to scare away the wolves before the flock could be eaten. Instead, they continued their work. Twice the boy had tricked them; they would not play the fool a third time.

The cry of warning had lost its significance. "Wolf!" was no longer a request for immediate help; it was the centerpiece of a new game, a game the villagers would always lose.

Not only in old fables do words undergo changes in meaning. Over time, through use, words take on new meanings so we must continually adjust our vocabularies lest we be caught saying the wrong thing. Consider the English word *nice*.[1] To its original meaning, "simple" or "ignorant," was added in the thirteenth century the sense "foolish" and "simple." Later, in the sixteenth century, "nice" would refer to "subtle" or "precise." But today, when we use the expression, "What a nice woman!", we mean none of these things.

Even in present time, words have widely divergent meanings. Does *light* refer to an object with little specific gravity, as in the expression "light as a feather"; to someone who is carefree—that is, lighthearted; or to a job that is easy to accomplish, "light work"? Or with the word *light*, do we mean "a source of light," as in the request, "Hand me that light, please"; "electromagnetic radiation visible to the eye"; or even "low in calories"?

The Gospel of Mark has its own word game, and it invites the reader to play along. The question Mark engages revolves around the identity of Jesus—or, specifically, what it means to call Jesus "Christ" and "Son of God." The related question is, What does it mean to be a disciple? For Mark, these two questions are inseparable: To have answered one is to have answered the other as well.

As with words such as *light* or *nice,* the key to determining what sense of a word is intended in a given discourse is the context in which the word appears. In some instances, the relevant context is provided by a sentence: Move away from the *light,* please. Is this package *light* enough for the two of us, or should we get help to carry it? In others, more context is needed. Thus *wolf* takes on new meaning in the context of the whole story. In the case of a story such as Mark's Gospel, the narrative *as a whole* also provides the data for our determination of the meaning of key concepts.

In this chapter, we will examine three central passages in the Gospel of Mark in order to explore how Mark understands the confession, Jesus is the Christ, Son of God. Our study will have immediate and far-reaching implications for our comprehension of discipleship in Mark, but these will be examined more carefully in subsequent chapters. The first crucial passage is Mark 8:27-33, where Peter confesses Jesus as the Christ.

THE JOURNEY BEGINS

The central section of Mark's Gospel is Mark 8:27–10:52. Mark highlights the importance of this section with three features. First, it is bordered on both sides by healing stories. The first is the two-stage healing of a blind person in Bethsaida (8:22-26). In our discussion of this passage in Chapter 2, we saw that this miracle story functions for Mark as a kind of parable of spiritual blindness, indicating the need for disciples to receive a "second touch" in order that they might lose their fuzziness of perception and understand better the significance of Jesus. The second healing story comes in 10:46-52, the healing of Bartimaeus, a blind beggar outside of Jericho. Unlike the blind man at Bethsaida, Bartimaeus sees clearly the first time. Moreover, unlike the first blind man, Bartimaeus, we are explicitly told, begins to follow Jesus on the way. That is, he not only regains his sight, he also becomes a disciple of Jesus.

Like a carefully selected picture frame, these two healing stories set off the profundity of the material Mark includes in 8:27–10:45. Somehow, within this frame, the perspective on Jesus' identity and the nature of discipleship is sharpened. It is as if Mark tells us to look here for a life-changing, eye-opening understanding of Jesus' significance. The message of this section leads to new levels of faith and faithfulness "on the way."

Second, the importance of this section is suggested by repeated references to Jesus' journey, his travel on "the way." Because the New Revised Standard Version does not always make this clear, we can list the relevant verses as follows:

- 8:27: "Jesus went on . . . and *on the way.* . . ."
- 9:33: "Then they came. . . ."
- 9:34: ". . . *on the way* they had argued. . . ."
- 10:1: "He left . . . and went. . . ."   .
- 10:17: "As he was setting out *on his way* . . ." (NRSV, "As he was setting out on a journey . . .").
- 10:32: "They were *on the way,* going up to Jerusalem . . ." (NRSV, "They were on the road . . .").
- 10:46: "They came. . . . As he and his disciples . . . were leaving Jericho, Bartimaeus . . . was sitting *alongside the way*" (NRSV, ". . . was sitting by the roadside").
- 10:52: "[He] followed him *on the way.*"

This cadence of references to "the way" in the company of other journey-related phrases recalls the references to "the way of the Lord" in Mark 1:1-3. These, in turn, invite us to remember earlier journeys in Israel's history, such as the Exodus trip, where God created and molded a new nation, the people God had redeemed. In the same way, this journey with Jesus is not a mere side trip for the disciples; they will receive instruction "on the way." Remembering the journey of Israel out of Egypt under God's guidance also underscores the divine purpose of Jesus' travel. Jesus is not traveling on "any" way; as 10:32 finally makes clear, he is on a particular road, the way to Jerusalem. This, we know, is the way that leads to betrayal, condemnation, death (10:32-34). More important, it is the way set before Jesus by God.

> The journey is the way of God. Being "on the way" means more than moving through a physical landscape to Jerusalem; it also means that Jesus moves toward the goal God has set before him: death in the service of proclaiming God's rule.[2]

Repeatedly, Mark notes that Jesus is not traveling alone; many are following him along the way, including the twelve disciples. Will they remain with Jesus on the way? Will they come to understand Jesus on their journey together? Only by following Jesus on the way will these questions be answered.

The third special sign in this section of Mark's Gospel is Jesus' repeated prediction of his suffering, death, and resurrection:

Then he began to teach them that the Son of Man must undergo great suffering, and be rejected by the elders, the chief priests, and the scribes, and be killed, and after three days rise again (Mark 8:31).

. . . he was teaching his disciples, saying to them, "The Son of Man is to be betrayed into human hands, and they will kill him, and three days after being killed, he will rise again" (Mark 9:31).

He took the twelve aside again and began to tell them what was to happen to him, saying, "See, we are going up to Jerusalem, and the Son of Man will be handed over to the chief priests and the scribes, and they will condemn him to death; then they will hand him over to the Gentiles; they will mock him, and spit upon him, and flog him, and kill him; and after three days he will rise again" (Mark 10:32-34).

Set against the backdrop of our previous examination of the first half of Mark's Gospel, these words of Jesus seem shocking. Where is the miracle worker now? Where is the one who controls demonic forces? Where is the teacher who amazes everyone with his authority? Where is the one who can raise a dead girl to life, whose spoken word brings healing?

This transformation of images is startling enough, but even more unexpected is the rationale Jesus gives for his anticipated suffering: "the Son of Man *must* undergo great suffering." Mark employs here the Greek word, *dei:* "It is necessary." Some have understood this as a necessity of divine fiat; Jesus must suffer because God has ordained it. A measure of truth resides in this understanding, but it must be carefully nuanced.

What we must not ignore is that the necessity of Jesus' sufferings arises in a particular time and place, a politically charged context in which people on the margins of society felt hopeless, powerless. Even righteous people had been pushed aside, marginalized, not only in spite of but sometimes because of their refusal to compromise their faith in God. In the arena of this sort of suffering, certain segments of Israel learned to affirm the necessity of suffering. Like them, Jesus understood that his sufferings were crucial to the drama by which God brings renewal and redemption. Innocent suffering is not void of meaning. As Martin Luther King, Jr. understood, and announced in his famous speech, "I Have a Dream!", the pain of the persecuted is efficacious in the drama of God's work in the world to bring peace and justice.

This means Jesus understood that his death would be effective in terms of God's redemptive purpose, though at this point in the story we are not told how this might be so (see Mark 10:45; 14:24). In this sense, his passion is willed by God, for Jesus' death would be the means by which God's will is revealed and realized.

At the same time, we should not downplay the human causes of Jesus' suffering. According to Mark 8:38, Jesus labeled the people of his day as an adulterous and sinful generation. The reference to adultery recalls John's charge against Herod, "It is not lawful for you to have your brother's wife" (6:18), and John's subsequent execution at the hands of Herod (6:19-28). What other fate might those who follow God in a wicked time receive? Jesus knew that suffering and death were the necessary consequences of his life because his allegiance was to the way of the Lord in the midst of a generation ruled by religious and political figures who did not follow that way.[3]

Set against the backdrop of these three features, Mark presents the dialogue between Jesus and his disciples about Jesus' identity. Here, the ruling question of the first half of the Gospel, Who is this man?, comes to a head.

A CRISIS OF MEANING

The first question addressed to the disciples, "Who do people say that I am?", is a question for outsiders. What is the public point of view? What do "those people" think? Previously, Mark has taken care to distinguish between insiders and outsiders. Insiders do the will of God; outsiders do not (3:31-35). Insiders have received the secret of the kingdom of God; outsiders can hear things only in parabolic form (4:11-12). We may know better who Jesus is, but for the moment the question revolves around what they think. "Who do people say that I am?" The disciples answer, "John the Baptist; and others, Elijah; and still others, one of the prophets" (8:28).

These examples of public opinion have already appeared in 6:14-15. Although wrong, these popular assessments of Jesus' person nonetheless have their significance. They show that Jesus is highly regarded by the people; they see in him no ordinary person. They regard him as a man of God, even if they are not aware of his true relationship to God. What of the disciples? Will they respond with bafflement, as before (4:41; 6:52)? Will they regard Jesus as no more than a great prophet?

Mark continues the story: Jesus asks, " 'But who do you say that I am?' Peter answers him, 'You are the Messiah.' And he sternly orders them not to tell anyone about him" (8:29-30). At last, we may think, someone within the story has recognized Jesus' true identity.

We know from Mark's introduction that Mark reckons Jesus as the Messiah or Christ, and the appearance of the title "Son of God" alongside Messiah in 1:1 and 14:61 suggests that he regards these titles as roughly equivalent. This would not be surprising; "Messiah" might have been understood, especially among people with a Jewish background, but would have been a puzzle to others. Son of God, then, would be roughly the equivalent of *Messiah* for a non-Jewish Greek audience. Hence, both the narrator (1:1) and God (1:11; 9:7) regard Jesus as Messiah, Son of God. Otherwise thus far in the narrative, only demons, who have supernatural insight, recognize Jesus in this way (1:24; 5:7). (Jesus silences them, however, for they choose only to name him, not follow him, as God's Son.) Now, speaking on behalf of the disciples, Peter acknowledges Jesus as Messiah; he aligns himself with God in his understanding of Jesus.

We are surprised, then, by Jesus' response to Peter. Rather than congratulating him on his newly found perception, he rebukes him. The New Revised Standard Version notes that Jesus "sternly ordered them," but the word Mark employs is even stronger. Elsewhere in Mark, the Greek term, *epitimaō*, is used to describe Jesus' rebuke of demons in the context of exorcisms (see, for example, 1:25; 3:12; 9:25).

How can this be? If Peter agrees with the narrator and with the divine voice in naming Jesus as Messiah, on what basis could Jesus rebuke him for his answer? At this point, we may recall our earlier discussion of Mark's "word game." Like the cry, "Wolf! Wolf!", or the words *nice* and *light*, *Messiah* is capable of a variety of understandings. We know that Mark affirms the messiahship of Jesus, but we know almost nothing about what this title means for him. He has had little to say about its content. In this passage, he is set on defining Messiah for us. Hence, though Peter may be using the correct words in affirming Jesus as Messiah, we are not sure that he understands correctly what it means for Jesus to be Messiah.

How did Peter understand this title, "Messiah"? One way to address this query would be to look into how this title might have been understood within first-century Judaism. Another approach might be to rehearse what we know of Jesus' identity from Mark 1:16–8:26. A third would be to concern ourselves more specifically with the present story in Mark 8 as it unfolds. Let us examine these in turn.

First, studies of first-century Judaism in the past three decades have underscored a variety of forms of Judaism in the Greco-Roman world. It is no longer possible to speak authoritatively of "what (all) Jews at the time of Jesus thought"—no more than it is advisable to generalize overmuch about varieties of Christianity or even Methodism at the end of the twentieth century.

If this is true of Judaism in general, it is also true of messianic speculation in particular.[4] First, among those first-century Palestinian Jews who reflected on Israel's deliverance from foreign occupation and hoped for the restoration of Israel, many seem to have had *no* messianic hopes at all. They anticipated no Messiah, no agent of salvation; God alone would come to establish peace and justice. In fact, references to a Messiah in the literature of this era are rare, and those that do exist are not altogether consistent in the career they outline for the Messiah. One particularly well-known passage from the first-century B.C. is worth citing, however:

> See, Lord, and raise up for them their king,
>   the son of David, to rule over your servant Israel
>   in the time known to you, O God.
> Undergird him with the strength to destroy
>   the unrighteous rulers,
>   to purge Jerusalem from gentiles
>   who trample her to destruction. . . .
> He will gather a holy people
>   whom he will lead in righteousness;
> and he will judge the tribes of the people
>   that have been made holy by the Lord their God . . . .
> There will be no unrighteousness among them in his days,
>   for all shall be holy,
>   and their king shall be the Lord Messiah.[5]

This text is striking for its clear delineation of the Messiah's role, though it must be admitted that other texts in which the title "Messiah" appears do not always agree with this one in their particulars. What is clear from this and related texts is the relation of the Messiah to the age of God's righteous rule. Here the Messiah is instrumental in implementing God's peace and justice. Elsewhere the Messiah might have a more passive role, but the Messiah is also cast in full revolutionary dress in other texts. It is not without some basis in the minds of people that, in the early second century, when Simon bar Kochba led a Jewish revolt against Rome, he could be acclaimed as "the king, the Messiah." Hence, even with the variety of notions about the Messiah in the first century, we would not be surprised if, when Peter hailed Jesus as the Messiah, he had in mind a savior figure who would implement the kingdom of God through the exercise of power against Rome.

Second, given Peter's knowledge of Jesus as available to us in the world of the story in Mark 1:16–8:26, what might Peter have intended by his confession, "You are the Messiah"? In Chapter 2, we saw how pervasive the theme of Jesus as miracle worker is for the first half of Mark's Gospel. He teaches authoritatively, controls demonic forces, heals the sick, stills the storm, walks on water, and raises the dead. What could Peter have in mind but some reflection of these experiences? He has been with Jesus from the beginning of his public ministry (Mark 1:16-20). He has witnessed his master's power; he has even exercised that power on behalf of Jesus (6:7-13). Surely, then, Jesus the Messiah must be Jesus the Powerful Healer, Jesus the Conqueror of Evil.

Third, we observed earlier that the key to understanding the meaning a speaker intends is the actual context of the utterance itself. What does the context of Peter's confession of Jesus at Caesarea Phillipi tell us about Peter's understanding of Jesus? The interaction between Peter and Jesus is controlled by a series of three rebukes. Thus:

Peter hails Jesus as the Christ (8:29).
Jesus rebukes Peter and the disciples (8:30).
Jesus teaches them that the Son of Man must suffer (8:31).
Peter rebukes Jesus (8:32).
Jesus rebukes Peter for setting his mind on human rather than divine things (8:33).

Throughout the Gospel of Mark, Jesus never uses the title "Christ" of himself; here, when Peter uses the term, Jesus seems to say, "Okay, you can call me 'Christ' if you want to, but let me define the terms." Jesus goes on to do so in terms of rejection and suffering. Peter, on the other hand, has his own definition of "Christ"; although we do not know all of the nuances he might attribute to this title, we do know this: In Peter's understanding, "Christ" and "suffering" do not go together. For him, "suffering Christ" constitutes a contradiction in terms.

In the end, Peter, who thought he was an "insider," with "insider knowledge," proves to be an "outsider." He knows the right words to use, but does not understand their meaning. Like the blind man at Bethsaida, he has some understanding, but his vision is still fuzzy; he cannot distinguish between people and walking trees. He needs something more.

Jesus springs a surprise on Peter and the disciples. But the reader is also surprised. As we hear Peter confess Jesus as the Christ, we nod our heads. Yes, Peter has it, we think to ourselves. The others were wrong—those outsiders who thought of Jesus as crazy (3:21), an agent of the devil (3:22), only a hometown boy (6:2-3), a mere prophet (6:14-16; 8:28). We want to identify with Peter, just as he aligns himself with God's own perspective on Jesus' identity. But Peter does not understand. This insider is still an outsider. He is still thinking like a mere mortal. He does not have in mind the ways of God. He does not have the secret of the kingdom. He does not understand Jesus and his mission. Do we?

Interestingly, Jesus proceeds from this redefinition of who he is to describe what it means to follow him: "If any want to become my followers, let them deny themselves and take up their cross and follow me" (8:34). In doing so, he draws the closest possible connection between the way of the Messiah and the way of the Messiah's followers. Both are oriented around the cross.

WHO SERVES WHOM?

A similar story appears at the end of this major section, in Mark 10:35-45. Unlike the dialogue in Mark 8:27-33, where the opening question centers on Jesus' identity, the initial question in 10:35-45 focuses on the meaning of discipleship. James and John come to Jesus with a request, "Grant us to sit, one at your right hand and one at your left, in your glory." Obviously, these two disciples take with utmost seriousness the promise of the resurrection of the Son of Man (10:34) and are planning ahead for their status in the new regime. In doing so, they have failed to notice what comes beforehand. Jesus' response is to redirect their attention to suffering and calamity, affirming that they will join him in his anguish (10:38-40). This question of political status has already surfaced in the confrontation between Peter and Jesus in Mark 8. Jesus is calling for a shift of giant proportions by pulling the rug from under a top-down, dominion-oriented philosophy of human relations. Leadership belongs to those who serve.

Jesus' own role is not to embrace power or allocate glory, but rather to serve. In this way, an inadequate view of discipleship leads to a climactic statement of Jesus' identity and mission: "The Son of Man came not to be served but to serve, and to give his life a ransom for many." In a profound but transparent melding of concepts, Jesus uses "slave language" to describe the role of the leader, and then he borrows the term "ransom" from the business of buying and selling slaves to describe the effects of his death. The way of servanthood has become the way of liberation.

These two encounters between Jesus and his disciples portray a consistent problem. Both Jesus and his disciples grasp the unfailing connection between the life of the Messiah and that of his followers, but they have widely divergent views of that life. The disciples, whose thinking is still all too earthbound, have in mind a powerful Messiah, a life of dominion and glory. They have no room for suffering and martyrdom in their definition of following God. Jesus, who has in mind the things of God, redefines power as service, and understands servanthood as the way God gets things done.

THE EXECUTION OF THE KING[6]

Thus far we have hinted that Jesus understands his approaching death to be integral to his identity and mission. This is nowhere better seen than in the crucifixion account itself. In Mark 14-15, Mark portrays Jesus' death as the moment of divine revelation.

This is the significance of the confession of the centurion at the moment of Jesus' death, "Truly this man was God's Son!" (15:39). God acclaims Jesus as God's Son at Jesus' baptism (1:9-11) and at the transfiguration (9:2-8). But the centurion is the first and only human throughout the Gospel to recognize Jesus as God's Son (15:39). What is more, Mark expressly notes that it is precisely as the centurion sees Jesus' dying breath that he makes his confession. Only in the cross is Jesus recognized rightly as the Son of God.

The place of Jesus' crucifixion at the heart of his divine mission is manifest in other ways, such as in the repeated association of passion events with Old Testament promise—such as in 14:21, 27, and the numerous ways Jesus is presented as the Suffering Servant of Isaiah 52:13–53:12 and the Suffering Righteous One of the Psalms. How Jesus' death functions as the center of God's redemptive plan comes to light in two other Markan texts, 10:45 and 14:24. In both passages, Jesus' death is interpreted as the basis of human salvation. In this ultimate act of service, Jesus lays down his life as an atoning sacrifice for the salvation of all. The irony of the scene of mockery at the cross may be understood along these lines also: Precisely by refusing to save himself, Jesus is able to save others (15:31; see also 8:35).

By refusing to follow their definitions of "Messiah" and exercise his power so as to escape the cross, Jesus demonstrates his messiahship (15:32). Especially important in this regard is the six-fold use of "king" with reference to Jesus (15:2, 9, 12, 18, 26, 32) combined with the three-fold mockery of Jesus on the cross (15:29-32). Condemned as a pretender to the throne, Jesus does have royal status, but not as we might have expected. His obedience to the divine mission, expressed preeminently in the cross—this is the ultimate mark of his royal identity.

CONCLUSION

Suddenly and decisively, the portrait of Jesus laid out in the first half of Mark's Gospel has been transformed. The confession of Peter in Mark 8 provides the occasion for the tables to be turned on the disciples, and on the reader. Like Peter, we have been taken with the activity of Jesus. We have learned to expect works of power from him.

And if this is our understanding of Jesus, what of our understanding of discipleship? Like Jesus, should not his disciples preach repentance, drive out demons, anoint the sick and heal them (6:12-13)?

But Jesus adopts a different point of view. Miracles are part of the picture. Resurrection is promised. But Jesus' agenda is to fulfill his divine mandate, God's commission given to him at his baptism. He is God's Son, and this means above all being obedient to God in sacrificial service, even when the way of God leads to Golgotha.

Questions for Reflection and Discussion

1. How do you answer Jesus' question, "Who do you say that I am?"
   How does your answer shape your lifestyle?

2. How do views of Christian living today echo messianic hopes in first-century Judaism?

3. What preconceptions today make it difficult to think about the Messiah as one who suffers?

4. What might "taking up the cross" mean today?

5. How might Mark's view of Jesus shape the mission of your church
   or fellowship?

CHAPTER FOUR

"COME, FOLLOW ME": THE CALL TO DISCIPLESHIP

> *As Jesus passed along the Sea of Galilee, he saw Simon and his brother Andrew casting a net into the sea—for they were fishermen. And Jesus said to them, "Follow me and I will make you fish for people." And immediately they left their nets and followed him. As he went a little farther, he saw James son of Zebedee and his brother John, who were in their boat mending the nets. Immediately he called them; and they left their father Zebedee in the boat with the hired men, and followed him* (Mark 1:16-20).

Three years ago I conducted an informal survey among twenty-seven pastors in my conference. I asked them four questions:

- How important to the Christian faith is the doctrine of the Incarnation, the belief that God became a human in Jesus of Nazareth?
- Who is the lay leader of the church you serve?
- How does this person spend his or her time, Monday through Friday?
- What difference does the doctrine of the Incarnation make to the everyday life of this lay leader?

The twenty-seven clergy with whom I spoke each affirmed the cardinal importance of the doctrine of the Incarnation. They represented a spectrum of theological commitments on a variety of issues, but spoke with one voice on the importance of the Incarnation to the Christian faith.

The lay leaders of the churches served by these pastors proved to be a varied group. Some were involved in health care, as nurses or physicians or occupational therapists. Others were business women and men, managers, and administrators. Still others were homemakers, lawyers, schoolteachers, construction workers, and retired.

What had the central doctrine of the Incarnation to do with the lives of these Christian professionals? Twenty-six pastors had no answer whatsoever for my question. They had either never considered the connection between the Incarnation and the lives of everyday people or, having thought about possible connections, were unable to articulate any such relationship. The twenty-seventh pastor replied, "Well, I suppose some of our most important doctrines have little practical relevance."

Illustrations of this tragic separation between theological affirmations and the day-to-day lives of those who make them could easily be multiplied. The pollster George Gallup regularly paints a picture of a Christian America, pointing out how many of us believe that Jesus Christ is the Son of God, hold to some vital belief in an afterlife, claim the Bible as God's Word, and so on. His data also demonstrate the distance between what many of us believe and what we actually allow to influence our daily lives. There is, for example, a vast difference between the number of persons who believe the Ten Commandments have relevance for today and the number of persons who can name more than four or five of them.

Affirmations of this sort, removed from the lives that might reflect them, are not the stuff of the Gospel of Mark. His story does not begin with an affirmation of Jesus' preexistence and incarnation like the Gospel of John. It is nevertheless true that for Mark what one believes about Jesus is determinative for how one behaves as Jesus' follower. There is for Mark the closest possible connection between who Jesus is and what disciples are to be. This is so much the case that we would be mistaken to suggest that Mark is concerned only or even primarily with "christology," a right understanding of the nature and mission of Jesus. Although Mark is concerned with this question, his story is motivated by concerns other than certifying that people cross their christological "t's" and dot their christological "i's." He believes that by presenting a more full-orbed portrait of Jesus' person and ministry, he will be able to transform the views of his audience on the nature of discipleship.

That discipleship is a primary concern for Mark is suggested in a number of ways, but especially by the way he has shaped the first half of the book. Between Mark 1:16 and 8:26 there are three major sections, and each begins by taking up the theme of discipleship. Thus, as the first section (Mark 1:16–3:12) is unveiled, Mark records the call to discipleship of Simon (Peter) and Andrew, James and John (1:16-20). This account of the call of the first disciples stands not only at the beginning of this subsection, however, but also as the head of the story of Jesus' public ministry as a whole. That is, *the first public act of Jesus is to call disciples.* Whatever else Jesus is about in the Gospel of Mark, he is concerned with the calling out of followers.

The second section (3:13–6:6) is also initiated by a passage taken up with the matter of discipleship. In this case Mark narrates the selection of the twelve apostles "to be with him, and to be sent out" (3:13-19). At the opening of the third section (6:7–8:26), Mark tells of the sending out of the twelve, two by two, to carry out the ministry of their master (6:7-13).

The importance of discipleship for Mark continues through the second half of the Gospel, 8:27–16:8, though in a different way. In this chapter, our focus will fall primarily on the first half of Mark's Gospel—especially on how Mark connected the meaning of discipleship with the person and message of Jesus. Later, we will see how Mark deepens this connection in the middle and final parts of his Gospel.

JESUS CALLS HIS FIRST DISCIPLES

In the opening episode of Jesus' public ministry, we are confronted with the intimate connection between who Jesus is as the Bringer of the Kingdom and the nature of discipleship. Four disciples are called, and their responses show the degree to which our encounter with Jesus can uproot our lives. Answering the call to follow Jesus places disciples on a road of sacrifice as they join him in service.

> As Jesus passed along the Sea of Galilee, he saw Simon and his brother Andrew casting a net into the sea—for they were fishermen. And Jesus said to them, "Follow me and I will make you fish for people." And immediately they left their nets and followed him. As he went a little farther, he saw James son of Zebedee and his brother John, who were in their boat mending the nets. Immediately he called them; and they left their father Zebedee in the boat with the hired men, and followed him (Mark 1:16-20).

Not only the *content,* but also the *location* of this story is important to our understanding of the meaning of following Jesus in Mark. We have already noted the position of this story at the beginning of Jesus' public ministry. As such, it communicates something fundamental about the nature of Jesus' mission: He has come to call together a community of followers. In a second way, however, the location of these events is important. The calling of Simon and Andrew, James and John follows immediately after Mark's summary of Jesus' proclamation of the kingdom of God in 1:14-15. This suggests the unavoidable connection between kingdom and discipleship, kingdom and community.

How is Jesus' kingdom announcement related to discipleship? After John is arrested, and is thus removed from the public eye, Jesus begins his open ministry, ". . . proclaiming the good news of God, and saying, 'The time is fulfilled, and the kingdom of God has come near; repent and believe in the good news'" (Mark 1:14-15). For Mark, this is the keynote of Jesus' proclamation. If we are to grasp Jesus' message in Mark, we must understand this summary.[1]

For Mark, Jesus' message is two-pronged: (1) He announces the kingdom, and (2) he calls for a response of faith and repentance. His message of the kingdom is rooted above all in the prophetic message of Isaiah, who anticipated the coming of God to bring *shalom,* peace and justice (Isa. 40). For Isaiah, the Lord God comes with power, to judge the world, and to show compassion to God's people. Isaiah prophesied,

> How beautiful upon the mountains
>   are the feet of the messenger who announces *peace,*
> who brings *good news,*
>   who announces *salvation,*
>   who says to Zion, *"Your God reigns"* (Isa. 52:7).

Here, the reign of God, God's kingdom, is peace *(shalom),* good news, salvation. This is the "good news of God" that Jesus proclaims. God's people have longed for the intercession of God in the world, the coming of the age of God's own reign, the epoch of peace.

According to Jesus, this long-awaited time is fulfilled; the kingdom of God has come near. Accordingly, in the ministry of Jesus, God has drawn near. But if God has come in sovereign power, this calls for a reconsideration of all other loyalties. If God has come in sovereign power, then all other commitments, all other claims for allegiance are moved into second place. This brings us to the other prong of Jesus' message in Mark, the call to discipleship.

The coming of God's reign in the world calls for response, and Jesus summarizes this response in the dual command, "Repent, and believe in the good news" (Mark 1:15). It is important to notice the sequence that Jesus outlines. Repentance and faith do not cause or bring the kingdom of God. Human response is not the source of the coming of God's sovereign rule. Rather, Jesus proclaims that a new day has dawned, a new time has come, a new way of understanding the world has broken into human existence. In light of this newness, people are called to embrace this newness in faith, and to reorient their lives around it. The kingdom of God has come near; *therefore,* repent and believe.

"Repent" and "believe": What are these responses? What do they imply? Mark could have constructed a dictionary-type definition or written an essay outlining the essential force of these concepts. But he did not. Instead, he opened the main body of his story of Jesus' life by telling a story of repentance and faith—the story of how the first disciples dropped their nets, left their boats, and followed Jesus. What do these two stories show us about the nature of discipleship?

From kingdom-proclamation to disciple-calling a decisive twist occurs. First, in Mark 1:14-15, Jesus proclaims the good news of God, the nearness of the kingdom, then calls for repentance and belief to *that* good news. Then, in Mark 1:16-20, response to the presence of God's sovereign rule is directed toward Jesus himself. "Repent and believe in the good news" becomes "follow me." One's stance in relation to the kingdom of God, then, is determined by one's response to Jesus. The connection between discipleship and the message of Jesus could not be stronger. Moreover, Mark develops this connection in ways that have not always been adequately recognized or appreciated.

Both stories of disciple-calling are told with minimal detail. This has led some readers to attempt a fleshing out of these stories. Looking between the lines, they have tried to reconstruct the story behind the story. They want to know, for example, the extent of the relationships between Jesus, Simon, and Andrew prior to the charge, "Follow me." Although stories like these often invite our imaginative engagement, in this case speculation of this sort misses the mark. Here and elsewhere, Mark wants to highlight the *abruptness* of the encounter together with the *immediacy* of the response. Rather than being invited to grapple with the psychology of the call to discipleship, we are challenged by the force of Jesus' presence, and we are shocked by the unencumbered obedience shown him by these fishermen. "As he went a little farther, he saw James . . . and his brother John. . . . Immediately he called them; and they left their father . . . and followed him."

Something else is shocking in this story. Although we are not immediately impressed with this, in these two narratives, the story line takes a surprising turn almost from the outset. At first, this account of a teacher with his disciples seems normal. After all, did not other Jewish teachers enter into student-pupil relationships? This is true, but entry into this association was generally on the basis of the pupil's initiative.[2] What does Jesus' initiative in this matter signify?

No doubt, Mark has in mind a reproduction in narrative form of the announcement of the kingdom in Mark 1:15. The kingdom of God breaks in as a divine act; the coming of salvation, of peace and justice, is not dependent first on human initiative. Neither is discipleship. As the Swiss New Testament scholar Eduard Schweizer observes,

> This makes it clear that the call as such is an act of grace, that it restores fellowship that has been broken, that forgiveness takes place here without anyone mentioning it and without any confession or penance or act of faith on the part of the person forgiven, because they are all implicit in what Jesus does.[3]

The call of discipleship breaks into the lives of these fishermen out of the blue, while they are "casting a net into the sea" or "in their boat mending the nets." This call is an act of grace.

We should also notice that the second prong of Jesus' message, "Repent, and believe in the good news," has its own echo in the story of the calling: "Follow me and I will make you fish for people." Two implications of this story are immediately clear: (1) The disciples are called to leave the economic security of their jobs; and (2) Even family ties are subordinated to the claims of the kingdom of God. As Peter affirms later, "Look, we have left everything and followed you" (10:28). The appearance of the kingdom of God relativizes all other relationships, all other commitments.

As radical as these two aspects of this response to Jesus' call may seem to us, there is more. Today in the West, changing jobs, even changing professions is more and more a matter of course. Even today, however, exceptions to this vocational mobility are known to us. In traditional fishing towns and villages along the North Sea in the northeast of Scotland, or in farming communities in the American Midwest, one's vocation is deeply rooted in the family and, indeed, in the social, religious, and political fabric of the local and regional communities. For such people, leaving boat and net or land and farming equipment is a departure from much more than economic stability. Departures of this kind would signify a departure from communal identity and tradition. Such people would be cutting themselves off at the roots, leaving a way of life deeply embedded in the substance of their rearing and their social world.

Jesus' call, "Follow me," thus upsets and overturns the world of those disciples. This is true for Simon and Andrew, who are portrayed by Mark as fishermen with no boat. As fishermen, they are relatively poor; they cast weighted nets into the lake while standing waist deep in the water. It is also true for James and John, who apparently are junior partners of a family business lucrative enough for the purchasing and upkeep of a boat and the hiring of day laborers. No doubt, their departure upsets their father Zebedee's plans for them eventually to assume full responsibility for the family enterprise.

Some interpreters have seen the response of these first four disciples as impractical, idealistic, irresponsible, and not to be repeated in "the real world." This way of thinking misses the mark, not least because the function of narrative cannot be reduced to interpretations that look for one-to-one reduplication in our world. Mark does not tell us these stories of call and response in order that we might copy the disciples. Rather, he is illustrating in their response the basic character of all true discipleship: a response to the presence of a sovereign God whose vision for peace and justice reaches the concrete realities of our personal, social, and economic lives. God's kingdom brings near an alternative vision of human existence in the world, calls for allegiance to this new reality, and makes it possible for people like James and John to embrace that new way. We may not be able to create from these stories a simple code for following Jesus, but we know this much: His call addresses us in our concrete, daily activities, and it looks to transform our priorities toward serving rather than being served.

Jesus thus calls them from one vocation to another. They will join their new master in the missionary endeavor. But this is an endeavor that must never be defined too narrowly. Jesus *is* talking about evangelism, but the character of this evangelism is shaped by the content of his own kingdom-preaching. The disciples are to join Jesus in calling people to respond to the presence of the kingdom *in the way that they themselves have responded*— by reorienting their whole lives around the breaking of God's peace and justice into the world. This reality is highlighted by the phrase Jesus uses to describe Simon and Andrew's new vocation: "fishers of people" (NRSV, "I will make you fish for people"). This language stems from a number of Old Testament texts, such as Jeremiah 16:16; Ezekiel 29:4-5; Amos 4:2. Here, "fishing" is used metaphorically to describe the role of those who warn Israel of impending judgment and call God's people away from their unfaithfulness. Disciples join Jesus, following him on the journey, as people who embrace the good news of the coming of God's kingdom into the world. And they call others to do the same.

A TOLL COLLECTOR FOLLOWS JESUS

A second story of Jesus' calling disciples repeats the theme of "leaving all," but also goes further. It pushes the meaning of the cost of discipleship to include the abolition of social comfort zones and protective barriers. Here Mark draws our attention to the call of discipleship as an act of grace, and shows that this grace extends even to undesirable people.

> Jesus went out again beside the sea; the whole crowd gathered around him, and he taught them. As he was walking along, he saw Levi son of Alphaeus sitting at the tax booth, and he said to him, "Follow me." And he got up and followed him.
>
> And as he sat at dinner in Levi's house, many tax collectors and sinners were also sitting with Jesus and his disciples—for there were many who followed him. When the scribes of the Pharisees saw that he was eating with sinners and tax collectors, they said to his disciples, "Why does he eat with tax collectors and sinners?" When Jesus heard this, he said to them, "Those who are well have no need of a physician, but those who are sick; I have come to call not the righteous but sinners" (Mark 2:13-17).

These two paragraphs in the Gospel of Mark are held together by a common theme, Jesus' extending friendship to people deemed unacceptable by society at large. Inasmuch as concerns with social boundaries were paramount in the pre-Christian and early Christian eras, these stories provide something of a window into first-century times. The events preceding the turn of the era moved the careful delineation of group boundaries to center stage for the Jewish people. Having experienced exile in the sixth century B.C. under Babylonian rule, then having been conquered by Alexander the Great in the late fourth century, having been persecuted horribly under Antiochus IV in the second, and having lived under oppressive Roman rule since the mid-first century B.C., the Jewish people were very conscious of the lines drawn between "us" and "them." In this sustained period of uncertainty, it was important to know "who is on our side."

Because various segments of Jewish society even within Palestine responded to the influx of Greek ideas and customs after Alexander the Great and to Roman rule in different ways, group differentiation took place even within the family of Jewish people. Outsiders might (and often did) include Jews, particularly those Jews who did not measure faithfulness before God in the same way as one's own "in group."

In this factional social setting, Jesus' behavior and the call to discipleship take on special significance. Clearly, Levi is an outsider, one of "them"; yet, Jesus receives him into fellowship as a follower.

The generally low status of toll collectors like Levi in the eyes of the general public in antiquity is well documented. Although some toll collectors were honorable, as a fraternity of people they were held in contempt by Jews and Romans alike. The second-century Roman historian Lucian puts them in the same category as adulterers, informers, and pimps. For the Jewish populace, this viewpoint would have rested in part on the fact that toll collectors were the point people in an oppressive system of taxation. Moreover, they were a constant reminder of Roman occupation of the Jews' home soil. For some, no doubt, toll collectors would have been implicated in perpetuating idolatry, since paying taxes to Caesar was tantamount to recognizing his (rather than God's) sovereignty in the land. More generally, toll collectors were scorned in society-at-large for their nosiness, and for their criminal activity. As a toll collector, Levi was a most unlikely disciple.

As before, when reading this account it is important that we not first attempt to get behind the story. Mark is unconcerned with issues related to Levi's spiritual journey before his encounter with Jesus. He provides no basis for psychological assessments related to how Jesus might have known ahead of time how Levi would respond. We have no knowledge of any prior meetings between Jesus and Levi. The story as Mark relates it provides no room for these questions. Using a terse economy of words, Mark relates, first, that Jesus invited Levi to a life of discipleship, followed by Levi's response: "He got up and followed him." Like James and John, Levi leaves the tools of his trade; in fact, he leaves everything and embraces a new way of life. He begins his journey with Jesus, following him on the way.

The second story, focused as it is on the banquet scene, serves to emphasize again the scandalous character of Jesus' ministry. Here the focus shifts from calling disciples to table fellowship, but the meaning of these acts overlaps. For Jesus' contemporaries, eating together was a profound social and religious symbol. Table fellowship signified acceptance and intimacy, the extension of a sense of family. Subsequently, persons might restrict their lists of acceptable eating partners to their own in-groups. This is clearly the expectation of the scribes of the Pharisees in this story. They ask, "Why does he eat with tax collectors and sinners?"

If tax collectors were scorned by society-at-large, what of sinners? The meaning of this term in the first century is not altogether clear. Some believe "sinners" refers to persons who deliberately adopted for themselves immoral lifestyles. Others observe that "sinners" is used in a more fluid way, to describe those who did not practice the Pharisaic program of holiness for Israel and so could not be trusted with regard to tithing and cleanness.[4]

More generally, in the social setting of first-century Judaism, focused as it was on social boundaries, a "sinner" could be one whose behavior departs from the norms of an identified group whose boundaries are established with reference to characteristic conduct.[5] In this way, "sinner" would be understood above all in terms of group definition. A "sinner" is an outsider.

Jesus extends the call to discipleship to a toll collector and then sits down to eat with tax collectors and sinners, outsiders all. We could hardly have a more forcible demonstration of God's gracious initiative. The call to discipleship is an act of grace that breaks into Levi's world. He is an outsider, but through the profoundly inclusive behavior of Jesus, Levi is made an insider. To this good news, he responds with "repentance and faith" (Mark 1:14), signified in his leaving his old life and embracing the new journey with Jesus.

THE APPOINTING OF THE TWELVE APOSTLES

A third story picks up where the first left off. In Mark 1:16-20, Jesus *invites* people to follow him and to take up his kingdom-oriented mission as their own. Now he *appoints* them to that mission. In this way, Mark emphasizes the close connection between the identity of the master and that of the disciples. They cast their lots with him and are designated to preach and engage evil forces just as he does.

[Jesus] went up the mountain and called to him those whom he wanted, and they came to him. And he appointed twelve, whom he also named apostles, to be with him, and to be sent out to proclaim the message, and to have authority to cast out demons. So he appointed the twelve: Simon (to whom he gave the name Peter); James son of Zebedee and John the brother of James (to whom he gave the name of Boanerges, that is, Sons of Thunder); and Andrew, and Philip, and Bartholomew, and Matthew, and Thomas, and James son of Alphaeus, and Thaddaeus, and Simon the Cananaean, and Judas Iscariot, who betrayed him (Mark 3:13-19).

The list of apostles Mark provides us is interesting in part because of its mysteriousness. We know that Jesus called others to discipleship—Levi, for example (2:13-14); why is he not included in this inner circle? More puzzling, perhaps, is that some persons are named here who have no role elsewhere in the Gospel. Clearly, apart from a select few—Peter, James, and John, for example—Mark is more interested in the appointment of apostles than in the apostles *as individuals*. This observation should encourage us to look carefully at the details of this process he does provide.

As in other stories in Mark, the geographical location of this event is important. The New Revised Standard Version correctly notes that Jesus has gone up a mountain (not "into the hills" as in some other translations). Although historians have debated which mountain this must have been, Mark seems more interested in its symbolic meaning. In many biblical passages, the mountain is a place of revelation, a meeting ground between God and humanity (see also Mark 9:2; 13:3). One Old Testament story is particularly apropos, that centered on the making of God's people at Mount Sinai in Exodus 20. This parallel passage comes to mind not only because of the reference to the mountain, but also because of the deliberate choice of *twelve* apostles. (Mark, in fact, tells his readers twice in this paragraph that there were twelve apostles appointed.) This number signifies the restoration of Israel in all its twelve tribes. Taken together, these two details show how the community forming around Jesus was interpreted against the backdrop of the redemption of Israel by God in the exodus from Israel and journey to a new land. Jesus, too, is forming a new people, oriented around the kingdom of God, whose purpose it is to restore Israel.

To what does he call them? On this, the structure of the passage is suggestive. Mark places in parallel two primary clauses describing the substance of apostleship and goes on to develop the second with two further descriptive clauses:

And he appointed twelve
   (1) to be with him, and
   (2) to be sent out
      (2*a*) to proclaim the message, and
      (2*b*) to have authority to cast out demons.

This way of visualizing the job description of the apostle is important, especially for North Americans today. Many people today, and several Bible translations of this passage, simply overlook the first purpose of Jesus' call, "to be with him." More important in our minds is doing, demonstrations of power. But for Jesus, the first priority is to be with him. This must not be taken in merely a spiritual or mystical way. These apostles are to join Jesus on his way, walk with him, eat and drink with him, listen to him, share hospitality with him, and be rejected with him. Their primary call is not to great achievements but to share life with him.

However, this focusing on Jesus always leads outward. Being *with* him leads to being *sent out by* him. When people become free toward God through their companionship with Jesus, they also become free toward the neighbor who needs them.[6] Unlike the pupils of the rabbis, Jesus' apostles are not training to become rabbis, to pass on a tradition or initiate new teaching. Jesus' disciples learn from Jesus through his teaching and through community with him to serve the kingdom of God. Having been shaped in their regular communion with Jesus, they are guided and empowered to proclaim the message of God's kingdom and to do battle against evil forces.

FAILURE AND GRACE

Other texts in Mark 1-8 help fill out the content of Mark's vision of discipleship. For example, in Mark 3:31-35 Jesus is in a house with an unidentified group of people whose chief characteristic is their obedience to God's will. They are Jesus' new family. Perhaps more well-known is the sending out of the twelve apostles in 6:7-13, anticipated already in the appointing of the twelve in 3:13-19. Empowered by Jesus, they are sent out to engage in missionary activity, placing before the people the radical claims of the kingdom of God and calling for a reorientation of life around God's just reign.

Less tied to specific discipleship-oriented passages, but nevertheless of a piece with that material, are the many ways the disciples fall short of the standard set before them. They are called to "follow Jesus," but they repeatedly demonstrate their incapacity to do so. They seem to leave everything, but repeatedly cling to old ways of thinking and acting. They are "with Jesus," but somehow fail to comprehend fully his significance. The most pressing warning of this kind appears in the list of Jesus' chosen twelve, where, finally, Judas is introduced as the one who betrayed Jesus (3:19). If one of the twelve is capable of betrayal, what of the "many" who followed Jesus (2:15)?

Significantly, Jesus warns the twelve of impending rejection; not all will welcome them into their homes (6:10-11). In Mark 6:1-6, Jesus himself is rejected in Nazareth, just like the prophets. So is John the baptizer

(6:14-29). Can the disciples expect anything less? Can they anticipate a different fate than the forerunner of the "Coming One" or of their Master? Rejection is not factored into their perceptions of discipleship, however. As Ernest Best observes, "Disciples are in danger of following Jesus but not perceiving that in following him they also must go the way of the cross." [7]

The theme of discipleship failure brings into even sharper relief the Markan accent on the graciousness of the call to discipleship. Mark reminds us that the initial call to follow Jesus, like the coming of God's kingdom, is not dependent on human response or faithfulness. Initial response to Jesus' invitation *initiates* a journey; it does not signal arrival. Disciples must learn from Jesus along the way. Along the way, too, they must work against evil in all of its guises and invite others to do the same.

We come to the end of this first half of Mark's Gospel wondering, though, if the disciples really understand. Do they really grasp who they are following? Are they really willing to leave aside old thoughts and old ways in order to cast their lots with Jesus?

Questions for Reflection and Discussion

1. Re-read Mark 1:16-20. If Mark were writing this story for twentieth-century people, how might he illustrate how Jesus' call addresses people in their concrete, daily lives?

2. How have you experienced the call to discipleship as a call of grace?

3. How has today's church allowed social boundaries to hinder the communication of the inclusive grace of God?

4. What costs have we learned to associate with Christian discipleship?

5. If Jesus' first disciples learned to be disciples indeed only by following him on the way, how do our own struggles shape us into greater Christlikeness?

CHAPTER FIVE

DISCIPLESHIP AS CROSS-BEARING

> [Jesus] called the crowd with his disciples, and said to them, "If any want to become my followers, let them deny themselves and take up their cross and follow me. For those who want to save their life will lose it, and those who lose their life for my sake, and for the sake of the gospel, will save it. For what will it profit them to gain the whole world and forfeit their life? Indeed, what can they give in return for their life? Those who are ashamed of me and of my words in this adulterous and sinful generation, of them the Son of Man will also be ashamed when he comes in the glory of his Father with the holy angels" (Mark 8:34-38).

THE WAY OF DISCIPLESHIP

The Journey

According to John Wesley, "If any teachings within the whole compass of Christianity may be properly termed 'fundamental,' they are doubtless these two—justification and the new birth." [1]

Justification speaks of that great work which God does *for* us in forgiving our sins. The new birth speaks of the great work which God does *in* us in renewing our fallen nature. What distinguishes Wesley's emphasis from born-again-ism in the twentieth century is the wider context in which he places it. The new birth is fundamental, but it is also only "the gate," "the entrance" into that new life in which we learn "inward and outward holiness."

> We might speak of the moment of birth as an instant, or at least a very short time. After that it takes a long time for the child gradually and slowly to grow, until the child reaches the stature of an adult. Similarly, a child is born of God in a short time, if not in a moment, but it is by slow degrees that the child afterward grows up to the measure of the full stature of Christ. [2]

In eighteenth-century Britain, where nominal Christian experience too often replaced growth in Christian character, Wesley learned to describe salvation as a process of "going on" to full salvation.

"Follow me," Jesus tells his disciples. With these words he invites people into a relationship over time, a journey, a process of growth. Thus, we might translate Jesus' invitation to discipleship in a way that reflects the continuousness of this relationship: Be about the business of following me!

Paul looked at the Christian life in a similar way, as in Colossians 2:6-7: "As you therefore have received Christ Jesus the Lord, continue to walk in him [NRSV, "continue to live your lives in him"], rooted and built up in him and established in the faith. . . ." Paul's use of the metaphor of "walking" for Christian discipleship brings to mind the description of the early Christian movement in the Acts of the Apostles as "the Way" (see, for example, Acts 9:2). And this emphasis is reminiscent of the theme of journeying we have already encountered in Mark's Gospel. "The way" into which Jesus invited his disciples, like Israel's journey to the promised land, is a time of training, transformation, a journey on which they might come to reflect to the world-at-large and in their lives together the character of God.

It may be more disappointing than surprising to the readers of the Gospel of Mark that the disciples of Jesus in Mark learn so slowly. Three times in Mark 8:27–10:52 we are told that Jesus informs his disciples of his forthcoming betrayal and execution. And each time one or another of the disciples misunderstands and responds inappropriately:

> *Mark 8:31-33*—After Jesus' first prediction, Peter rebukes him, only to be told that he has in mind human, not divine things.
> *Mark 9:30-32*—After Jesus' second prediction, ". . . they did not understand what he was saying and were afraid to ask him."
> *Mark 10:32-35*—Along the way, they were amazed and afraid. After Jesus' third prediction, James and John begin requesting positions of honor.

The disciples do not understand; they need something more. Mark's initial readers might have been disappointed by this, but probably not surprised. After all, as we will see, they themselves were apparently missing some of the pieces to this puzzle. Their own circumstances had created for them a crisis of faith. Life in the world was not going according to their plan; indeed, life seemed to have turned against them. How could they, followers of a miracle-working, popular Messiah, encounter so much pain? They needed help, insight, a deeper appreciation of life on the way.

In Mark 8:27–10:52, Mark hopes to open up to his audience new dimensions of discipleship. This would happen *on the way*—a reality signaled best by the broad structure of this section. As we have seen, immediately preceding this section is the story of a blind man (8:22-26), whom Jesus heals in a two-stage process. He requires a second touch in order to see clearly. At the close of this section is the account of Bartimaeus, a blind man who, having been healed by Jesus, follows Jesus on the way (10:46-52). Mark uses this framing or sandwiching device frequently to help make his point. Thus:

(A) The Two-Stage Healing of a Blind Man (8:22-26)
   (B) Instruction for Disciples on the Way (8:27–10:45)
(A¹) The Healing of a Blind Man (10:46-52)

and:

(A) Jesus' Family Comes to Take Him Away (3:21)
   (B) Jesus Accused of Working with Satan (3:22-30)
(A¹) Jesus Redefines Family (3:31-35)

or:

(A) Jesus Curses a Fig Tree (11:12-14)
   (B) Jesus Cleanses the Temple (11:15-19)
(A¹) The Withered Fig Tree (11:20-21)

In each case, Mark tells his stories in this way in order to guide our understanding. In Mark 3, Mark shows that the appropriate way to respond to Jesus' mission is by joining the family of those who do the will of God. In Mark 11, the withering of the fig tree and the failing of the temple both point to the new way of faith and life that Jesus offers those who follow him. In Mark 8-10, this same storytelling technique shows that, on the way, Jesus will be healing the vision of the disciples, clearing their minds of misperceptions, pointing them on the way forward to authentic discipleship. Thus, the *way* of discipleship is precisely *the life of following*, the journey, joining Jesus on the way.

The Community

Given our own tendencies to make faith a private and individual matter, we should note explicitly one further ingredient of the way of discipleship for Mark. It is easy for us to tell stories of leaving family and friends to get in touch with who we really are, or to relate how our decisions on issues of morality are personal, therefore ours alone to make. Such thinking, however, would have been alien to the first-century readers of Mark's Gospel. The African proverb, "We are, therefore I am," much more faithfully represents the style of self-perception in the Roman world. Not without good reason do we read that Jesus sent his disciples out for ministry in pairs (Mark 6:7-13). "Two-by-two" suggests something profound about the first-century individual. An individual would have been understood in relation to others, not on his or her merits alone.[3]

Hence, Jesus' invitation to discipleship is a call into a community of disciples. Interestingly, toward the end of the central section of Mark, which is our focus in this chapter, Peter declares to Jesus, "Look, we have left everything and followed you." Jesus' reply signals that those who "leave" will be given much more in return, and one of the primary features of the gifts awaiting disciples is "brothers and sisters, mothers and children" (10:28-31). Just as Jesus redefined family in Mark 3:33-35 as those who do the will of God, so here he places the life of discipleship squarely within the new family, the community of Jesus' followers.

TAKING UP THE CROSS

After Jesus foretold his own maltreatment at the hands of the Jewish leaders (Mark 8:31), he went on to draw an intimate connection between his fate and that of all would-be followers. Both disciples and the unevangelized masses receive the same call; Christian discipleship allows for no first- and second-level distinctions, as though some receive a higher or deeper call than others. Instead, everyone is invited to an uprooted existence wherein loyalty to Jesus and service in God's kingdom take precedence over all counterclaims. Jesus proclaims (Mark 8:34-38),

> If any want to become my followers, let them deny themselves and take up their cross and follow me. For those who want to save their life will lose it, and those who lose their life for my sake, and for the sake of the gospel, will save it. For what will it profit them to gain the whole world and forfeit their life? Indeed, what can they give in return for their life? Those who are ashamed of me and of my words in this adulterous and sinful generation, of them the Son of Man will also be ashamed when he comes in the glory of his Father with the holy angels.

So removed are we from the social and political realities of first-century Roman rule that the language of cross-bearing is often lost on us. "Everyone has a cross to bear," we are told, usually with reference to the conflicts of everyday existence. For Mark and his readers, these everyday struggles might have seemed almost trivial. After all, in the first-century Palestinian world, "taking up the cross" would have had a very specific historical referent. "Taking up the cross" was a preamble to crucifixion, and crucifixion was a form of execution reserved for persons found guilty of opposing the state.

Mark wrote his Gospel with some form of persecution in mind; this is suggested by two observations. First, the language of Mark 8:34-38 reminds us of a courtroom scene, where people might be called upon to *deny* their relationship to Jesus, who was himself executed as an insurrectionist, a pretender to the throne (Mark 15). As Mark records elsewhere, judicial hearings before Jewish and Roman leaders are the expected lot of believers (13:9). Interrogations and other courtroom-like situations provide disciples with opportunities to save their lives or lose them (8:35), to acknowledge their loyalties to Jesus or turn away from him and the gospel in shame (8:38). For such persons, to declare loyalty to Jesus would be tantamount to denying themselves in an ultimate way (8:34).

Second, as the German New Testament scholar Martin Hengel has shown, evidence within the Gospel of Mark points to the conclusion that it was written in a time of severe distress, in the late A.D. 60s, before the fall of Jerusalem in 70.[4] Although most New Testament scholars now agree that we must rethink earlier pictures of empirewide persecution of Christians in the first century, ample evidence does exist for more localized anti-Christian sentiment and activity. According to Hengel, Mark was writing to Christians who were experiencing just such a persecution. A conclusion of this nature is confirmed by references to the persecution of the disciples in Mark 10:38-39, and by the ominous warning in 13:13: "you will be hated by all because of my name."

In other words, we should not romanticize Jesus' definition of discipleship as "taking up the cross." By inserting the word *daily* in his form of this saying—"If any want to become my followers, let them deny themselves and take up the cross *daily* and follow me"—Luke shows that later in the first century and in a different locale he and his community came to understand this saying in a metaphorical way (Luke 9:23). No such interpretation is suggested by Mark, however. He is giving witness to the ultimate cost of identification with Jesus and his message. Of course, in the 60s, not all followers of Jesus faced martyrdom under Nero—nor did all those martyred face death via crucifixion. Hence, Jesus' words should not be taken as simply a prediction of heinous death. Instead, in this way, women and men who would be disciples were informed at the outset of the possibility of overt hostility because of their faith. Likewise, they heard in no uncertain terms about the necessity of single-minded identification with Jesus' redemptive message and mission.

Mark's readers, faced with persecution and malice, needed to be reminded of their primary commitment. Even in a world without executions of this nature, cross-bearing retains today something of its crucial importance. Followers of Jesus then and now must be clear about their loyalties. They must beware competing claims from professional life, wealth, political institutions, family, social security, even from one's own concerns with honor and status—claims that assert themselves over against the coming of God's kingdom into the world.

A QUESTION OF STATUS

If followers of Jesus in Mark's day had a problem with suffering, rejection, and persecution, it was in part because they expected more for themselves. The reign of God was breaking into the world; should this not have wide-reaching implications for those who follow the Bringer of the kingdom?

Who Is In—Who Is Out

Christians were not the only ones in the first-century Mediterranean world who were concerned with matters of privilege. Considerations of honor and status were integral to the general social fabric. Ancient concerns with status were not, however, entirely like related concerns in the United States today. Since the Industrial Age, Americans generally have been keenly aware of their status in the community as measured above all by relative wealth and abundance of possessions. We have operated with notions of status that revolve around definitions of class and class situation. And the basic categories of class situation are property and lack of property.[5]

Status was equally at issue in the Greco-Roman world, but the standard of measure was different. References to "middle class" as those who make their living through acquired skills or from their limited property had little meaning in the apostolic era. This is true above all because the level of one's wealth was of little consequence except insofar as that wealth might be translated into status honor. For example, Zacchaeus, known to us from Luke 19:1-10, was a wealthy man, but, because of his profession as a toll collector, he was an outsider in his own community.

In the first-century Roman world, status was measured especially with reference to belonging, to being counted as "one of us," to being regarded as "in." Belonging to the inner circle might require a certain level of wealth, but money and possessions were not nearly as important as other factors—for example, being born into the right family, ethnicity, gender, religious purity, vocation, and educational background. First-century folk wanted to know who was "in," who was "out"; who was "us," who was "them." Group definition and boundary lines between *us* and *them* were carefully maintained. Hence, it was important to measure relative goodness and loyalties. And it was important to know *who* was important, who was further "in" than you, who deserved greater honor and service.

One of the clearest examples of this concern with boundary definition in the central section of Mark's Gospel is narrated in Mark 9:38-40:

John said to [Jesus], "Teacher, we saw someone casting out demons in your name, and we tried to stop him, because he was not following us."

But Jesus said, "Do not stop him; for no one who does a deed of power in my name will be able soon afterward to speak evil of me. Whoever is not against us is for us. For truly I tell you, whoever gives you a cup of water to drink because you bear the name of Christ will by no means lose the reward."

Apparently, the disciples believe they have found a way to control the community of Jesus' followers; they can claim for themselves greater status honor because of their intimacy with Jesus as signified by their use of his name. Are they not the ones whom Jesus sent out to have authority over unclean spirits (Mark 6:7)?

So great is their arrogance in this context, that John objects that this stranger is not a follower of *us*. John wants to be followed, rather than be a follower! The irony of this attempt at boundary-making is that the disciples, through their spokesperson Peter, have already demonstrated their failure to understand the name they so freely claim as their own (8:27-33). They are concerned with right language; Jesus seems more interested in right behavior, serving those who bear the name of Christ (9:41). They want a formal definition of "us," "the inner circle of disciples"; he is looking for people who behave in a way that signals their decision to follow him in a life-transforming, evil-defeating life.

Elsewhere in this section, especially with reference to welcoming children, attempts to occupy seats of honor, and discussion of wealth, similar concerns with status and boundaries are at work.

Are You a Child?

On two separate occasions, Jesus brings children to center stage in order to instruct his disciples on the nature of their life together. In the first, he contrasts the disciples' jealous maneuverings with the welcoming of a little child (9:33-37). In the second, he contrasts the reception of the kingdom of God by a child with the inability of a wealthy man to enter the kingdom (10:13-31). Both stories have been interpreted in a variety of ways by modern students of Jesus and the Gospels, particularly because of our modern tendency to romanticize childhood and our consequent failure to appreciate how Jesus' words might have been heard in the first century.[6] Children could be found at the lowest rung of the ladder of honor and status in the first-century Mediterranean world. They might be valued for their potential upon achieving adulthood or for the assistance they provided in family industry. However, they were not yet adults and were viewed as irrational and without judgment; hence, they had little if any intrinsic value as human beings. This accounts for the widespread practices of child abandonment and even infanticide by which family size was sometimes regulated.

Such practice may seem foreign and barbaric to us in the United States at the end of the twentieth century. Our public values honor the idea of "youth." Agencies that represent us work on behalf of the rights of children. The United Nations Educational, Scientific, and Cultural Organization (UNESCO) has called ours the "century of the child." [7] Are we not a child-centered society? In fact, our rhetoric on this matter has far outdistanced our practice. Our infant mortality rate is higher than thirty-three other countries. By failing to deal with far-reaching social and economic needs in our cities and among our young, we inadvertently have come to depend on abortion as a principal means of dealing with crisis pregnancies. We have created an economic system that demands long hours spent away from the home for both parents. Many one-parent families live beneath or hover at the edge of the poverty line, often without substantive help from the non-custodial parent. What is more, as the Associate Provost of Southern Methodist University, Leroy Howe, has observed,

> . . . the final irony, and obscenity, in a child-centered society, is that child abuse is widespread and on the rise. . . . The terrified eyes of vulnerable young—and of the parent charged with their protection—portend the assaults to come, and the psychic wounds a lifetime cannot heal. [8]

We, then, are not so far from being able to understand just how topsy-turvy Jesus' message must have sounded for his disciples. In Mark 9, they are arguing over who among them is the greatest. This is tantamount to arguing who among them is worthy of receiving honor from the rest. Jesus turns this way of thinking on its head, insisting that the primary issue is not who receives honor from the rest, but who gives honor to the least. "Welcoming" has to do with showing respectful service. Jesus asks his disciples to reorient their thinking about status and honor, to understand that the greatest honor is extending respectful service to those with no status at all, to the powerless, to those whom society-at-large largely overlooks. "Whoever welcomes one such child in my name welcomes me," Jesus says, "and whoever welcomes me welcomes not me but the one who sent me" (9:37).

We see this way of thinking again in Mark 10:13-16. Here Jesus observes that the kingdom of God belongs to people like the little children. It is also present in Mark 10:41-44, where Jesus scolds his disciples for adopting the way of the Gentiles: "You are thinking like humans again!" we can almost hear him say (see 8:33). *They* lord it over each other, but *you* prove your greatness, your status, your membership in this community by taking up the role of the servant. "Servants" waited on tables, washed the feet of their superiors, and performed other assignments deemed inappropriate for males who were born free or whose freedom had been granted.

It may be that even these acts of service could be rationalized for free people *if* they were directed toward people of higher status. This, however, is not Jesus' point. Instead, service is to be directed toward "all" (9:35; 10:44), including little children (9:36-37). "The result is that Jesus turns things upside down; he teaches that true greatness means giving yourself in personal service to one from whom you can receive no benefit in return."[9]

Are You Rich?

The question of wealth and its relation to discipleship in the Gospel of Mark is raised most clearly in Mark 10:17-27. Here, the issue is developed along two lines, first in an encounter between Jesus and an anonymous man seeking eternal life and then in conversation between Jesus and his disciples:

> As [Jesus] was setting out on a journey, a man ran up and knelt before him, and asked him, "Good Teacher, what must I do to inherit eternal life?" Jesus said to him, "Why do you call me good? No one is good but God alone. You know the commandments: 'You shall not murder; You shall not commit adultery; You shall not steal; You shall not bear false witness; You shall not defraud; Honor your father and mother.'" He said to him, "Teacher, I have kept all these since my youth." Jesus, looking at him, loved him and said, "You lack one thing; go, sell what you own, and give the money to the poor, and you will have treasure in heaven; then come, follow me." When he heard this, he was shocked and went away grieving, for he had many possessions.
>
> Then Jesus looked around and said to his disciples, "How hard it will be for those who have wealth to enter the kingdom of God!" And the disciples were perplexed at these words. But Jesus said to them again, "Children, how hard it is to enter the kingdom of God! It is easier for a camel to go through the eye of a needle than for someone who is rich to enter the kingdom of God." They were greatly astounded and said to one another, "Then who can be saved?" Jesus looked at them and said, "For mortals it is impossible, but not for God; for God all things are possible."

Like the earlier passages regarding children and the kingdom of God, this story has received many interpretations, most along one of two approaches. A number of scholars have attempted to read this story as a simple denunciation of wealth and as a call to total renunciation of wealth by Jesus' followers today. In their understanding, a wealthy Christian is a contradiction in terms. Others have found here a less concrete, more metaphorical challenge. Jesus, they say, is calling women and men to put aside whatever gets in the way of following Jesus. The key to reading this story, however, is the initial question about relative "goodness" and the astonishment of the disciples following Jesus' response.

Why does this person address Jesus as "Good Teacher," and why does Jesus refuse this title? Is Jesus really calling into question his own goodness? More probable is that Jesus questioned the assumptions and values this man had in mind as he introduced the conversation. "Good," in this first-century world, would have been determined above all by concerns with status honor; thus, it would have meant "deserving," "in," "one of us." Hence, this anonymous seeker is approaching Jesus with flattery, no doubt hoping for a compliment in return. Such exchanges of greetings would have been normal fare among status equals in the Mediterranean world. Far from following the normal social conventions of his day, however, Jesus refuses any involvement with such behavior. "Goodness" is not determined for Jesus by human-drawn boundaries between insiders and outsiders. "Goodness," as he will go on to demonstrate, is not a function of relative wealth or morality. In fact, of themselves, neither will guarantee entry into the kingdom of God; what is more, possessions make such entry even more difficult.

This is the reality that has the disciples reeling in astonishment. No doubt, like many in their culture, they had been well schooled in the common belief that good things come to good people. No doubt, they would also be familiar with an important corollary: People with good things must be good people. As a wealthy man, a man with property, is this anonymous person not deserving of honor from Jesus; is he not a candidate for successful admission into the kingdom? Add to his wealth his own admission of his blamelessness with regard to keeping the commandments, and the disciples can come to no other conclusion but that this fellow is an insider; surely he belongs in the company of the kingdom.

Jesus, however, has already determined the credentials of kingdom-seekers. They are known by their selfless service to all, including little children. They are known by their fundamental allegiance to the kingdom of God, with its concerns for peace with justice. They are known by their joining Jesus in a mission that actively opposes all forms of resistance to the kingdom of God. And now they are known by their concrete solidarity with the marginalized of this world, those of low status, the forgotten folk at the bottom of the ladder of status honor. These are the sorts of people being formed *on the way.*

THE GOAL OF DISCIPLESHIP

Having read Mark 10:32-34, we know that the path on which Jesus is leading his disciples goes to Jerusalem. There, "the Son of Man will be handed over to the chief priests and the scribes, and they will condemn him to death." It is on *this* way that Jesus instructs his disciples as to the shape of authentic discipleship. Does this mean, however, that Jesus' own goal is also the culmination of discipleship? Jesus must face Golgotha; must Jesus' disciples likewise face violent execution? What is the way of the cross?

In the time of Mark's writing his Gospel, just as in countless times and places since, martyrdom has been a reality for those who walk the way of Jesus. Readers of Mark are challenged to come face-to-face with this possibility. The ultimate denial of self in the face of imprisonment and death for the sake of Jesus and the gospel is always and everywhere within the scope of the meaning of authentic discipleship.

Likewise, in the A.D. 60s, just as throughout the history of Christianity, millions of followers of Jesus have not been confronted with this choice. Hence, although "the way of the cross" embraces martyrdom, it has not always culminated in hostility; "the way of the cross" means more.

This "something more" is signaled later in the Gospel, when Jesus anticipates his going to Galilee to meet his disciples after his resurrection (14:28; see also 16:7). A cross awaits Jesus in Jerusalem, but the story of the disciples will continue. They will, like him, proclaim the in-breaking kingdom in word and deed, calling others to new commitments, new allegiances, a radically new orientation of life. They will, like him, refuse human-oriented values that revolve around status and that motivate the drawing of boundaries in ways that exclude others who are working on behalf of the kingdom of God. They will, like him, relate their lives directly to "outsiders," however such persons might be defined—with respect to economics, gender, ethnicity, and so on. And he will be *with* them, now in his resurrection (Mark 14:28; 16:7), just as they were called to be *with* him in the beginning (Mark 3:14).

In significant ways, then, the goal of discipleship is the journey itself; that is, the journey is open-ended, so that the mission of the disciples is always to be joined and the challenge to further growth in discipleship is always present. Rabbis may take on disciples in order to produce more rabbis, but Jesus calls disciples to shape them as his disciples and to enlist them in the ongoing work of producing more disciples.

For Mark, however, the journey will not extend into perpetuity. The journey has an end. The journey of the community of followers comes to an end when Christ returns. "The journey takes believers on a path of suffering and persecution but also on a path of mission. When mission has been fulfilled and the gospel has been preached to the nations (13:10) then comes the end of all journeying."[10]

Questions for Reflection and Discussion

1. In what ways is Mark's picture of discipleship as a journey helpful to you? Challenging?

2. To what degree have you experienced discipleship as a community enterprise?

3. How might claims from professional life, political institutions, wealth, and family compete with serving the in-breaking kingdom of God?

4. "Jesus asks his disciples to reorient their thinking about status and honor, to understand that the greatest honor is extending respectful service to those with no status at all, to the powerless, to those whom society-at-large largely overlooks." How might this portrait of discipleship work its way into your local church or fellowship? Into the marketplace?

5. Write down some additional thoughts at this time about what it means to "take up the cross" today.

CHAPTER SIX

THE COMMUNITY OF DISCIPLES:
WATCHING AND WALKING TOGETHER

> *As for yourselves, beware; for they will hand you over to councils; and you will be beaten in synagogues; and you will stand before governors and kings because of me, as a testimony to them. And the good news must first be proclaimed to all nations. When they bring you to trial and hand you over, do not worry beforehand about what you are to say; but say whatever is given you at that time, for it is not you who speak, but the Holy Spirit. Brother will betray brother to death, and a father his child, and children will rise against parents and have them put to death; and you will be hated by all because of my name. But the one who endures to the end will be saved* (Mark 13:9-13).

In Scandinavian mythology, "Ragnarök" refers to the end of the world. Demon forces will rise up and prevail against the gods. Moral chaos will invade the world of humanity. The sun will be veiled as the earth is swallowed up by the sea.

Intertestamental Judaism developed its own version of the coming doomsday. Tribulation and catastrophe would precede the end. A similar perspective has found expression in a number of movies in the 1970s and '80s. As documented in such films as *Apocalypse Now* and *The Day After*, North Americans have developed their own sense of impending doom in the midst of the nuclear-war anxiety of the post-Vietnam era.

Though Scandinavian and late-Jewish thinking provided for a new world following the cataclysmic destruction of the old, they also had a common pessimistic tendency. People often associate the coming of the end with feelings of profound pessimism, experiences of widespread upheaval, and great suffering.

In a surprising way, the Gospel of Mark addresses pessimism of this sort. The presence of pain had created a dilemma for Jesus' disciples. Had God deserted them? Were they mistaken to follow this man from Galilee? Are they really God's people? Is this the end? Are these trials the prelude to Jesus' triumphant return? Mark's Gospel is concerned with how Jesus' disciples respond to suffering—especially, but not only, that arising out of persecution.

Throughout the Old and New Testaments, the problem of pain is often on display, at other times near the surface. Some have called this "the only problem," yet it is disconcerting to see how slowly the church has drawn on the resources of interpretation available in scripture. We often fail to appreciate the perspective on suffering provided by a biblical book such as Mark's Gospel. Here important questions are raised about suffering—both by Mark's audience and by the Gospel writer himself.

Having oriented ourselves to the heart of Mark's instruction on the nature of Jesus' person and mission and on the intimately related subject of the character of discipleship in Jesus' way, we may now move to what is a central concern for the last chapters of Mark: how discipleship is centered around the cross of Christ.

IS THIS THE END?

In the late fourth century B.C., Alexander the Great occupied Palestine on his way to conquering the then-known world. In his wake he left seeds for the growth of Greek ideas and the influx of Greek culture among the Jewish people. This was to determine the shape of Judaism in subsequent centuries. Thus, during the period just prior to the birth of Jesus of Nazareth and into the early Christian era, we may trace two basic streams within Judaism. On the one hand, many Jews, especially priests and others of wealth and powerful status, looked upon the influx of Greek ideas and language into Palestine as a political steppingstone. Likewise, they saw in the Roman occupation of Palestine an opportunity to consolidate their own positions and assert themselves as God's leaders for a new day. On the other hand were those marginalized people for whom Greek ways and Roman rule had come to spell religious and social disaster. While those who embraced the Greek way of life and who flirted with Rome were rewarded for their cooperation and loyalty, others lost their ancestral homes, their freedom, their status in Palestinian culture, and their human dignity.

For these latter people, hope more and more focused on the future. Today was lost; present life had soured. Even if God might be working in the present to bring about God's purpose, that purpose could only be realized in the future, beyond history. The world was beyond repair. Rather than renewing the world, God would have to replace it.

A number of ancient Jewish writings predict the end of the world as a time of tribulation. The time of the end and of the inauguration of the new epoch would be a time of woe. This, they say, would be a time of earthquakes, war, and famine. Widespread persecution and friends betraying friends—this would be the stuff of the tribulation accompanying the death of the old world and the birth of the new.[1] Christians living in the late A.D. 60s would have been faced with selective persecution in the Roman Empire, the temptation to join the Jewish people in the violent struggle against Rome, and the general intensification of hostilities in Palestine before the fall of Jerusalem in A.D. 70. Against the backdrop of late-Jewish expectation of the distress prior to the end, Christian disciples in this period would quite naturally have developed a heightened sense of anticipation: Is this the end? This seems to be the concern behind Mark's record of Jesus' discourse on the signs accompanying the end of the age in Mark 13.

Modern-day Christians have a love-hate relationship with Mark 13. Some, concerned with timetables for the end of history have turned to this chapter for data to help them interpret "the signs of the times." For them, Mark 13 is a code book for interpreting the front page of today's newspaper in the context of God's redemptive plan. Others find this chapter strange, otherworldly, with no clear points of contact with life as we live it today.

When reading a text such as Mark 13, perhaps the most important thing to remember is that what seems mysterious to us at the end of the twentieth century was not always so. In this chapter, Jesus is speaking the language of first-century Palestine, with words and images shared with those marginalized people whose hope for a better world resided in God's direct intervention. There are, in fact, a number of examples of this form of speech, called an apocalyptic discourse, within late Judaism.[2]

According to Mark,

> As [Jesus] came out of the temple, one of his disciples said to him, "Look, Teacher, what large stones and what large buildings!" Then Jesus asked him, "Do you see these great buildings? Not one stone will be left here upon another; all will be thrown down."
>
> When he was sitting on the Mount of Olives opposite the temple, Peter, James, John, and Andrew asked him privately, "Tell us, when will this be, and what will be the sign that all these things are about to be accomplished?" (Mark 13:1-4).

These first four verses set up the topic of Jesus' subsequent address. Jesus' disciples, all from rural environs, marvel at the magnificence of the temple, which was enlarged in the late first century B.C. to reflect its role as the center of significant wealth and industry. Herod's Temple embodied much of the grandeur of other major buildings shaped by Greek architecture. Jesus' opening salvo is both a critique of the wealth-and-power system behind the temple and a promise that God would transform the topsy-turvy society on which it was based. Peter, James, John, and Andrew hear his words as a prediction of the destruction of the temple *and* of the end of the world. "What will be the sign that all these things are about to be accomplished" (13:4)? Underlying their question is their belief that God would provide a sign as a portent of the coming of the end. They inquire, How will we know?

Jesus' answer, against the backdrop of similar discussions in the first-century Jewish environment, is in many ways expected and normal. He refers to the proliferation of savior-figures who, unlike Jesus, emphasize showy signs and miracles (compare Mark 8:11-12 with 13:6, 21-22; Deut. 13:1-3). He mentions wars, both near and far away ("rumors of wars"), as well as natural disasters, like earthquakes and famines (13:7-8). These, however, do not signify the end; rather, they are the distresses, the woes that accompany the breaking of God's kingdom into the world.

The conflict between good and evil, light and darkness, of which these woes are expressions, carries over into the political and religious arenas. Earlier, Jesus had urged would-be disciples to consider the cost of identification with his mission—the potential forfeiting of life itself (8:34-37). Now he fills in the content of this threat:

> "they will hand you over to councils; and
> you will be beaten in synagogues; and
> you will stand before governors and kings
>   because of me, as a testimony to them" (13:9).

No stone will be left unturned in the prosecution of the faithful. This does not necessarily refer to a coming, intensive, empirewide persecution of Christians because of their faith in and confession of Christ. No evidence for this sort of phenomenon in the first century exists. Jesus' warning does not disallow, however, the presence of active hostility toward Christians on more localized bases in cities and regions throughout the Empire. Jesus even went so far as to anticipate the fall of Jerusalem and the final crisis.

By and large, Jesus' words thus far would have sounded typical in his environment. He spoke like most any other prophetic figure in the first-century Jewish context. In one way, however, his speech departs significantly from similar addresses. With a repeated refrain, he brings to the fore a new theme:

"Beware that no one leads you astray" (13:5).
"As for yourselves, beware . . ." (13:9).
"But be alert . . ." (13:23).
"Beware, keep alert . . ." (13:33).
"And what I say to you I say to all: Keep awake" (13:37).

His disciples ask, "When will this be, and what will be the sign that all these things are about to be accomplished?" Jesus answers not with *a* sign, but with sign*s* that mark the birthing of God's kingdom into the world. They ask, "When will this be?" He replies, twenty-seven verses later, "No one knows . . . but only the Father" (13:32). Other prophets might and often did give speculative timetables about the end. Jesus takes an altogether different approach. For him, "being in the know" was superseded by being faithful, by being prepared. Watchfulness, prayer, steadfastness—this was the appropriate response to oncoming trial.

This message is twice underscored in the unfolding drama of Jesus' passion in Mark 14. After his Last Supper, Jesus went with his disciples to Gethsemane (14:32-42). There, he sought God's will in prayer while they fell asleep. The central message of Mark 13—Be alert! Keep watch!—is thus echoed negatively in Jesus' question to his sleepy disciples: "Simon, are you asleep? Could you not keep awake one hour?" In the face of hostility, persecution, and disaster, the disciples exemplify the wrong response: sleep (14:37, 40, 41). Later, "one of those who stood near drew his sword" (14:47); this, too, is inappropriate. In the midst of persecution, only Jesus demonstrates faithful behavior. He prays. He waits to discern God's way. Then he acts on his understanding of that purpose with firm resolve. He practices what he has preached. Stay awake, he says. He stays awake.

A second example of Jesus' command to alertness appears in Mark 14:53-72. This is the narration of Jesus' hearing before the Jewish council and Peter's triple denial of Jesus in the courtyard of the high priest. Like a modern-day screenwriter, Mark weaves these two stories together in order to show their close relationship:

- Jesus is taken to the house of the high priest (v. 53).
- Peter sits with the guards in the courtyard of the high priest (v. 54).
- Jesus is indicted by the Jewish council (vv. 55-65).
- Peter denies Jesus three times (vv. 66-72).

When asked to identify with Jesus, Peter denies ever having known him. Jesus had remarked that disciples must deny themselves; Peter denies Jesus. Jesus' faithfulness in the midst of the Jewish hearing stands in sharp contrast to Peter's failure in the face of prospective hostility. Remembering the Gethsemane episode, we should not be surprised by this contrast. Oriented around God's purpose, having embraced God's design in prayer at Gethsemane, Jesus is able to face his opponents with resolve. Peter, having slept through the night, is unsure of God's purpose; he has no insight into God's story or his role in it. Hence, faced with this informal "hearing" around the courtyard fire, he curses and swears an oath, exclaiming, "I do not know this man you are talking about."

The difficult historical circumstances of the A.D. 60s provided fuel for many kinds of doubts and temptations. Some might have found the impetus for a retreat into end-time speculation, an escapism oriented to the future. Others might have heard the rebel call to arms, to join the violent revolution against Rome; after all, was this not the final battle of light against darkness? But Jesus accepts neither of these hasty conclusions. Instead, he observes, "The end is still to come. . . . This is but the beginning of the birthpangs" (13:7). And he proposes an alternative: Not least in times of conflict and persecution, followers of his way must *continue in his way*. They must continue to stay awake, keeping their eyes and ears open to the sights and sounds of God's kingdom (Mark 4). They must realize that present events have deep meaning before God and that these events provide opportunity for the extension of the mission to all nations (13:10).

MAKING SENSE OF SUFFERING

Nevertheless, for those who thought faithfulness to God would put them on the winning side of history, growing hostility and the onset of persecution are a puzzle. Suffering often makes people take personal inventory: What have I done wrong? Am I really one of God's people? The First Letter of Peter addresses people undergoing an identity crisis of this kind: "Beloved, do not be surprised at the fiery ordeal that is taking place among you . . . as though something strange were happening to you" (4:12). Mark has a similar viewpoint, even if he develops it in a vastly different way. The approach of 1 Peter is based on a comparison between Jesus and Christian disciples: Jesus is the precious, living stone rejected by others, chosen by God; so also you are "chosen and precious in God's sight," living stones rejected by others (2:4-10). As we have seen, Mark identifies the closest imaginable relationship between the mission and fate of Jesus and that of his disciples. This concern runs much deeper than we have been able to study thus far, however. With respect to suffering, Mark's concern reaches its zenith in Mark 13-15.

Mark 13 shows clearly that the suffering of the church in history is integral to the birth pangs of the coming of God's kingdom. In Mark 13, Jesus declares that the church will participate in the woes that lead to a new era of peace and justice. When will the church suffer in this way? With a fascinating maneuver, Mark shows that the passion of the church *has already begun in the final suffering of Jesus*. That is, the suffering of the church is wrapped up in the suffering of the Messiah. How does Mark make this connection? He shows that what Jesus predicted of the church (Mark 13) has already begun to happen to Jesus himself (Mark 14-15)—as follows:

Mark 13	Mark 14-15
Jesus predicts the destruction of the temple (13:2).	Witnesses accuse Jesus of threatening to destroy the temple (14:58); at Jesus' death, the temple veil is split in two (15:38).
Jesus predicts that the disciples will be delivered up to religious and political authorities (13:9-13).	Jesus is himself delivered up to Jewish and Roman authorities (14:10, 11, 18, 21, 41, 42; 15:1, 10, 15).
Jesus predicts that disciples will be betrayed by those with whom they share intimacy (13:12-13).	Jesus is betrayed by one of the Twelve, an intimate, one with whom he has shared table fellowship (14:10, 20, 43).
Jesus predicts that "in those days" . . . "the sun will be darkened" (13:24).	At Jesus' crucifixion, "darkness came over the whole land" for three hours (15:33).
Jesus predicts that the Son of Man will be seen coming in clouds with great power (13:26).	At his hearing before the Jewish council, Jesus affirms the coming of the Son of Man seated at the right hand of the Power, and coming with the clouds of heaven (14:62).
Jesus observes that no one knows the hour (13:22, 33 ["time," NRSV]).	At Gethsemane, Jesus proclaims that the time has come (14:32-42).
The disciples are to watch (13:5, 9, 23, 33, 35, 37).	At Gethsemane, the disciples fail to watch (14:34, 37, 38).
In 13:35, Jesus says, "Therefore, keep awake—for you do not know when the master of the house will come, in the evening, or at midnight, or at cockcrow, or at dawn."	Throughout 14:17–15:1, these same time designations—evening, midnight (that is, at the third watch), and early morning—are used.
Jesus describes the actions of the master of the house: He comes and finds you sleeping (13:36).	At Gethsemane, Jesus came and found the disciples sleeping (14:37-38).

These parallels demonstrate one important approach for interpreting Jesus' death: On the cross Jesus inaugurated the coming of the new world. What is more, the persecution of Jesus' disciples must now be interpreted in the same way. Far from being a contradiction of their status as God's people, the hostilities they experience certify their status.

Is Mark interested only with the suffering of Christians; or only with that suffering that comes to them because of their faith? He is concerned with these forms of suffering, but Mark 13 expands the field of vision to include the pain of the *whole world*. Wars and famines and earthquakes are no less tragic for their being understood as expressions of the labor pains by which the kingdom appears. For Mark, these calamities are not to be celebrated or embraced as "inevitable in God's purpose"; he does not wink at pain. Mark does affirm, however, that the distress of the world is not without purpose. Its meaning is derived from the greater mural of God's work by which he is ushering in a new day, a day of no tears. Nothing is forgotten.

In other words, Mark invites his readers to understand suffering within the wider context of God's purpose from creation to new creation. Our lives and these painful realities are located in God's story—the God who does not leave us alone with pain.[3] In this way we may grasp the depth of George MacDonald's observation: "The Son of God suffered unto the death, not that [we] might not suffer, but that [our] suffering might be like his."[4]

COMMUNITY AND SUFFERING

As we have repeatedly observed, Mark is not concerned with suffering in the abstract. "The problem of pain" is not his problem. Neither is it ours here. We have raised the question of suffering for one reason only—because Mark himself raises it. And Mark raises it because of the painful experiences and prospects of his audience. How shall they understand their suffering? Mark observes that suffering finds its meaning within the context of the in-breaking kingdom of God. But there is more.

In suffering, Mark's audience is reminded of another aspect of life-contexts: the family. This connection comes to the fore directly for Mark in 10:28-30. Following the interchange between Jesus and his disciples about the possibility of entry into the kingdom for the rich,

> Peter began to say to him, "Look, we have left everything and followed you." Jesus said, "Truly I tell you, there is no one who has left house or brothers or sisters or mother or father or children or fields, for my sake and for the sake of the good news, who will not receive a hundredfold now in this age—houses, brothers and sisters, mothers and children, and fields with persecutions—and in the age to come eternal life.

At the outset, Peter's confession is reminiscent of his call to discipleship in

1:16-18. Although he left nets, not fields, and seems to have maintained continued and close relations with his family (see 1:29-31; 1 Cor. 9:5), he has reoriented his whole existence around following Jesus. Jesus does not deny this, but interprets it as a "leaving" that is not without its reward.

Following Jesus is not a get-rich-with-God scheme, as though following Jesus brings with it automatic material prosperity. The addition of the phrase, "with persecutions," here guarantees this. Instead, Jesus promises (1) identification with Jesus in the cross and (2) a new family.

This is not the first time Mark has underscored the import of the community of faith. In Mark 1, Jesus calls people into a new kinship group—out of the community of their lives as fisher-folk, into the community of his followers. In Mark 3, Jesus calls apostles to be "with him," and then he redefines the family. He insists that the operative characteristic of mothers, brothers, and sisters is obedience to God. Now, in Mark 10, he asserts that one of the primary blessings of discipleship is a new way of being family.

Notice the members of the family as identified by Jesus:

Mark 3:35	*Mark 10:30*
brother	brothers
sister	sisters
mother	mothers
	children

Interestingly, in these passages, husbands and fathers are not mentioned. In addition, mothers are known for their role as child-bearers, not as wives to their husbands. This is consistent with Mark's more general critique of a top-down authority structure dominated by men who seek seats of honor and powerful status (see 10:35-45). This new way of being family gives pride of place to egalitarianism, caring rooted in the values of the kingdom, leadership that focuses on the needs of the least. God is the only Father in Mark's Gospel, and this God is defined not by the poor examples of first- (or twentieth-) century family life, but by the loving sacrifice of Jesus, God's Son.

There is something deliberate about this concentration on the family of faith in a Gospel concerned with discipleship oriented around the cross. The "way of the cross" is never a way for individuals, but always for the people called. For Mark, questions of identity and meaning must be answered fundamentally in relation to the community of the faithful. As the United Methodist ethicist Stanley Hauerwas has observed, Christians historically have had no "solution" to the problem of evil. "Rather, they have had a community of care that has made it possible for them to absorb the destructive terror of evil that constantly threatens to destroy all human relations."[5]

As Mark understands them, hostility and violence have the potential to fragment the community. Alone, Judas betrays Jesus. Alone, Peter denies not himself, but Jesus. But Jesus promises more. Following his execution on the cross, he will join the disciples in Galilee. In resurrection power, he will reconstitute the community of disciples. Together again, and with him, they will have the challenge to carry on the mission of Jesus in the service of the kingdom. Will they remember the centrality of the family of disciples to this mission? Will they have come to terms with the way of the cross? Will they? Will we?

Questions for Reflection and Discussion

1. Jesus' words, "Be alert! Keep watch!," play a major role in the Gospel of Mark. How can we put them into practice today?

2. How does Mark's interpretation of the role of suffering surprise or challenge you?

3. In light of Mark's Gospel, how might Jesus' suffering shape your view of your own pain? Of the suffering of our world?

4. Using what you have learned from the Gospel of Mark and drawing on your own ideas and experience, what might a community of
   sacrifice look like today?

5. Name some specific and concrete ways that your congregation can function as a community of redemptive suffering.

ENDNOTES

Preface

1. In the West, the most vocal skeptic must be G. A. Wells, who argues that Christian, Roman, and Jewish references to Jesus and his death are all fictitious (see, for example, *The Historical Evidence for Jesus* [Buffalo, New York: Prometheus, 1982]). His canons for historical veracity, if consistently applied, would deny us any knowledge of antiquity. For a more positive, nuanced approach to the evidence for Jesus, see A. E. Harvey, *Jesus and the Constraints of History* (Philadelphia: Fortress, 1982).

2. Joel B. Green, *The Death of Jesus: Tradition and Interpretation in the Passion Narrative*, WUNT 2:33 (Tübingen: J. C. B. Mohr [Paul Siebeck], 1988).

3. The term *narrative* is subject to a wide variety of uses today. For our purposes, the term is interchangeable with *story,* or with an account which has the characteristics of a story.

Chapter One

1. Charles Taylor, *Sources of the Self: The Making of the Modern Identity* (Cambridge, Massachusetts: Harvard University, 1989), 495.

2. See Stanley Hauerwas, *Naming the Silences: God, Medicine, and the Problem of Suffering* (Grand Rapids, Michigan: Wm. B. Eerdmans, 1990), 39-95 [56].

3. Codex Bezae is followed in this innovation by selected Old Latin manuscripts, though each in its own way.

4. See Martin Hengel, *Crucifixion in the Ancient World and the Folly of the Message of the Cross* (Philadelphia: Fortress, 1977).

5. Geza Vermes, *Jesus the Jew: A Historian's Reading of the Gospels* (Philadelphia: Fortress, 1973), 131; see pages 130-40.

6. See 4QpNah 3-4.1.7-8; 11QTemple 64.6-13. These and other relevant data are discussed in Joseph A. Fitzmyer, S.J., "Crucifixion in Ancient Palestine, Qumran Literature, and the New Testament," in *To Advance the Gospel: New Testament Studies* (New York: Crossroad, 1981), 125-46.

7. *Gospel of Peter* 5.19.

8. See, for example, Leon Morris, *The Apostolic Preaching of the Cross,* 3d. ed. (Leicester: InterVarsity, 1965); *idem, The Cross in the New Testa-*

ment (Grand Rapids, Michigan: Wm. B. Eerdmans, 1965); John R. W. Stott, *Cross of Christ* (Downers Grove, Illinois: InterVarsity, 1986).

9. This paucity of evidence for the atonement in the Gospel of Luke and the Acts of the Apostles is especially noteworthy because (1) Luke is responsible for approximately 25 percent of the New Testament writings, and (2) Luke still emphasizes the centrality of Jesus' death in God's redemptive purpose. This should lead us to ask, What further significance does the death of Jesus have?

10. See, for example, Martin Hengel, *The Atonement: The Origins of the Doctrine in the New Testament* (Philadelphia: Fortress, 1981).

11. Some people today find "kingdom" a troublesome, even offensive translation of the Greek term *basileia,* and prefer phrases such as "dynamic rule of God" or "reign of God." Although I am not insensitive to this concern for gender-inclusive language, these alternative phrases are themselves misleading with regard to the content of the message of Jesus. Somehow, the ideas of "reign" and "realm," both of which are captured by the Greek term *basileia,* must be conveyed. See Joel B. Green, *Kingdom of God: Its Meaning and Mandate* (Lexington, Kentucky: Bristol, 1989).

Chapter Two

1. See Mary Ann Tolbert, *Sowing the Gospel: Mark's World in Literary-Historical Perspective* (Minneapolis: Fortress, 1989), 303-04.

2. The common Jewish formula for a scriptural citation, "as has been written . . . ," links the citation to prior material not subsequent material. See Robert A. Guelich, *Mark 1-8:26,* WBC 34a (Dallas, Texas: Word, 1989), 10.

3. For example, T. Dan 6:4 (first or second century B.C.): Satan ". . . knows that on the day in which Israel trusts, the enemy's kingdom will be brought to an end" (H. C. Kee, "Testaments of the Twelve Patriarchs: A New Translation and Introduction," in *The Old Testament Pseudepigrapha,* 2 vols., ed. James H. Charlesworth (Garden City, New York: Doubleday, 1983/85), 1:810; T. Sim. 6:2-7 (first or second century B.C.): where a vision of the age of peace is introduced with the conditional clause, "If you divest yourselves of envy and every hardness of heart . . ." (Kee, "Testaments," 787); T. Jud. 23:5 (first or second century B.C.): redemption is promised after ". . . you return to the Lord in integrity of heart, penitent and live according to all the Lord's commands" (Kee, "Testaments," 801).

4. See also 1:28, 37, 45; 2:12; 3:20; 4:1; 5:20, 21, 24, 42; 6:33-34; 7:24, 36-37.

5. See Green, *The Death of Jesus,* 148-56.

Chapter Three

1. This illustration is borrowed from Peter Cotterell and Max Turner, *Linguistics and Biblical Interpretation* (Downers Grove, Illinois: InterVarsity, 1989), 131.

2. David Rhoads and Donald Michie, *Mark as Story: An Introduction to the Narrative of a Gospel* (Philadelphia: Fortress, 1982), 64.

3. See Tolbert, *Sowing the Gospel,* 202; Ched Myers, *Binding the Strong Man: A Political Reading of Mark's Story of Jesus* (Maryknoll, New York: Orbis, 1988), 242-43.

4. See J. H. Charlesworth, "From Jewish Messianology to Christian Christology: Some Caveats and Perspectives," in *Judaisms and Their Messiahs at the Turn of the Christian Era,* ed. Jacob Neusner, William Scott Green, and Ernest S. Frerichs (Cambridge: Cambridge University, 1987), 225-64.

5. *Pss. Sol.* 17:21-32. English translation from R. B. Wright, "Psalms of Solomon," in *The Old Testament Pseudepigrapha,* 2:667.

6. On what follows, see Joel B. Green, "Death of Jesus," in *Dictionary of Jesus and the Gospels,* ed. Joel B. Green, Scot McKnight, and I. Howard Marshall (Downers Grove, Illinois: InterVarsity, forthcoming).

Chapter Four

1. I have explored this further in Green, *Kingdom of God: Its Meaning and Mandate,* written for a general readership.

2. This and other distinctions between Jesus and the rabbinical model are explored in Martin Hengel, *The Charismatic Leader and His Followers* (Edinburgh: T. & T. Clark, 1981).

3. Eduard Schweizer, *Jesus* (London: SCM, 1971), 40.

4. See Marcus J. Borg, *Conflict, Holiness and Politics in the Teachings of Jesus, Studies in the Bible and Early Christianity 5* (Lewiston, New York: Edwin Mellen, 1984), 84.

5. See James D. G. Dunn, "Pharisees, Sinners, and Jesus," in *The Social World of Formative Christianity and Judaism: Essays in Tribute to Howard Clark Kee,* ed. Jacob Neusner, et al. (Philadelphia: Fortress, 1988), 264-89 (275-76).

6. Schweizer, *Jesus,* 41.

7. Ernest Best, *Mark: The Gospel as Story, Studies of the New Testament and Its World* (Edinburgh: T. & T. Clark, 1983), 85.

Chapter Five

1. John Wesley, "The New Birth," in *The New Birth: A Modern English Edition,* ed. Thomas C. Oden (San Francisco: Harper & Row, 1984), 1.

2. Wesley, "The New Birth," 16-17.

3. See further, Bruce J. Malina, *The New Testament World: Insights from Cultural Anthropology* (Atlanta, Georgia: John Knox, 1981), 51-70.

4. Martin Hengel, "The Gospel of Mark: Time of Origin and Situation," in *Studies in the Gospel of Mark* (London: SCM, 1985), 1-30.

5. See, for example, Max Weber, *Economy and Society: An Outline of Interpretive Sociology,* 2 vols., ed. Guenther Roth and Claus Wittich (Berkeley: University of California, 1968), 1:302; see 1:302-07, 2:926-32; *idem, The Theory of Social and Economic Organization,* ed. Talcott Parsons (New York: Free, 1947), 424-29.

6. On this issue I am grateful to my former student, Lynne M. Kellems, who made her research on "Jesus and the Children: Interpretations in Mark 9 and 10" available to me.

7. On this and what follows, see Leroy T. Howe, "Between the Generations: Healing the Hurts and Reconciling the Differences," *PSTJ* 43 (1, 1990), 1-18; especially pp. 7-10. I have determined the world ranking of the United States of America with regard to infant mortality from the "Comparative National Statistics" on "Vital Statistics, Marriage, Family," in *1990 Britannica Book of the Year,* ed. Daphne Daume (Chicago: Encyclopedia Britannica, 1990), 780-85.

8. Howe, "Between the Generations," 8.

9. Dennis M. Sweetland, *Our Journey with Jesus: Discipleship according to Mark* (Wilmington, Delaware: Michael Glazier, 1987), 64.

10. See Best, *Mark: The Gospel as Story,* 92.

Chapter Six

1. These texts are listed and discussed in Dale C. Allison Jr., *The End of the Ages Has Come: An Early Interpretation of the Passion and Resurrection of Jesus* (Philadelphia: Fortress, 1985), 5-25.

2. See John J. Collins, *Daniel with an Introduction to Apocalyptic Literature, The Forms of Old Testament Literature* 20 (Grand Rapids, Michigan: Wm. B. Eerdmans, 1984).

3. Hauerwas, *Naming the Silences,* 66-67.

4. George MacDonald, quoted in C. S. Lewis, *The Problem of Pain* (New York: Macmillan, 1962), 7.

5. Hauerwas, *Naming the Silences,* 53.